MW00855988

# Hide

# YOUR

# GUNS

ঙ০ল

## OFF-GRID

## SURVIVAL CACHES

### BY

## SAM ADAMS

A PRODUCT OF SOLUTIONS FROM SCIENCE

Hide Your Guns: Off-Grid Survival Caches
©2011 Solutions From Science

## Notice of Rights

Manufactured in the United States of America. All rights reserved. No part of this book may be reproduced in any form or by any electronic or mechanical means, including information storage or retrieval systems, without permission in writing by the copyright owner. For more products by Solutions From Science, please visit us on the web at www.solutionsfromscience.com

## Notice of Liability

The information in this book is distributed on an "as is" basis, for informational purposes only, without warranty. While every precaution has been taken in the production of this book, neither the copyright owner nor Heritage Press Publications, LLC shall have any liability to any person or entity with respect to any liability, loss, or damage caused or alleged to be caused directly or indirectly by the instructions contained in this book.

Unless otherwise noted, scripture quotations are taken from the Complete Jewish Bible, Copyright © 1998 by David H. Stern and published by Jewish New Testament Publications, Inc., Clarksville, Maryland. All rights reserved.

## Published by:

Heritage Press Publications, LLC
PO Box 561
Collinsville, MS 39325


ISBN 13: 978-1-937660-01-7

ISBN 10: 193766001X

Heritage
Press
Publications

# CONTENTS

INTRODUCTION

.................................................................... 4

CHAPTER ONE

Security Systems ......................... 8

CHAPTER TWO

Simple Hiding Places ...................... 19

CHAPTER THREE

Elaborate Hides ....................... 25

CHAPTER FOUR

Weapons Caching ...................... 32

CHAPTER FIVE

Preparing a Cache ...................... 38

CHAPTER SIX

Concealing a Cache ...................... 52

CHAPTER SEVEN

Metal Detectors ...................... 58

CHAPTER EIGHT

Staying Below the Radar ...................... 64

CHAPTER NINE

A Biblical Response to Self-Defense,
Guns, and 2nd Amendment Rights ...................... 70

CHAPTER TEN

Conclusion ...................... 79

RESOURCES FOR MATERIALS

.................................................................... 82

IMPORTANT RESOURCES: PRODUCTS FOR SELF-RELIANT LIVING

.................................................................... 83

IMPORTANT RESOURCES: BOOKS AND DVDS

.................................................................... 90

# INTRODUCTION

*If it's time to hide your weapons,*
*it's time to dig them up.*
Anonymous

History teaches us about dictators and tyrants who disarmed their people and began an ethnic cleansing program against various segments of their populations. The Holocaust is but one example.

These practices aren't just historical events however, but policies that continue even today in the countries we send our soldiers to fight in and the places we read about in the headlines of our newspapers.

China, Rwanda, Burma, Uganda, Somalia, Darfur are examples of oppressive regimes that have disarmed their citizens and killed millions. Government thugs routinely rape, steal, and disenfranchise millions more.

England, Canada, Europe, Australia, Mumbai, and various communities in the United States—countries and areas that have denied their citizens the right to keep and bear arms, and have subjected them to increasing lawlessness and helplessness in the face of criminal predators and terrorists.

With our government turning over more of its authority to international courts and global regulations, the United Nations Human Rights Council's position that a person has no legal right to self-defense becomes even more chilling. That the council seats are stacked with representatives from nations with the worst human rights violations on record is even more telling.

They are the governments that deny their citizens basic self-defense measures while at the same time imprisoning and killing their own people.

ॐ

In addition, treaties entered into with foreign countries supersede American law and the Constitution. Our government doesn't have to take away our Second Amendment rights.

They only have to sign a UN treaty to effectively disarm the American people.

All that sounds scary and threatening, but what does it mean for those of us at home, just trying to get by with our day-to-day lives, raising our families, and doing the best we can?

Ask the people of Britain and Wales who, despite stringent gun control laws, suffer the highest probability of becoming a victim of crime. Ask the people of Australia, Canada, Europe, and Scandinavia who have been disarmed. They will more likely become victims of a confrontational crime than those of us in the United States.

*Up to 3.6 million crimes are averted each year by the presence of a firearm.*

Burglars in areas that do not restrict people's access to guns are cautious about entering a home that's occupied. They hesitate to rob mom and pop privately owned stores and instead target national chains because they know that corporate rules keep employees from defending them-selves with a weapon.

According to a National Center Policy Analysis brief, criminals commit 10 million violent and 30 million property crimes a year in the United States. John R. Lott, author of the book *More Guns, Less Crime*, says that guns are used to hinder up to 3.6 million crimes a year.

Gun control advocates would like you to believe that easy access to guns is the reason for our crime rates in the United States, yet in Vermont, a state with no restrictions on gun ownership or carry laws, the rate of homicide and robbery is a fraction of the national rate for these crimes.

ဆၥလ

In this time of economic unrest, when we see the value of our money and our homes decline and when our jobs hang by a thread, maintaining a home defense and security system against people who would come and steal what little you have is a must.

The courts have ruled, all the way up to the Supreme Court, that the police have no constitutional obligation to protect American citizens from criminals. Let me put that another way: the police don't have to save you from any crime being committed against you. If you want to protect your family and possessions, you're going to have to do it yourself.

The goal of this manual is to provide you with the information you need to put together a plan for hiding your weapons and valuables from anyone who would want to steal them from you. Only you can decide what you want to hide and to what extent you want to hide it.

Don't let apathy or an attitude of "it can't happen in this country" keep you from getting your affairs in order now. The time to be prepared is before the need arises.

If you wait until the thief is at the door, it'll already be too late.

Find out just what people will submit to, and you have found out the exact amount of injustice and wrong which will be imposed upon them; and these will continue until they are resisted with either words or blows, or both. The limits of tyrants are prescribed by the endurance of those whom they oppress.

Frederick Douglass

# CHAPTER 1
## SECURITY SYSTEMS

*But now, he said, if you have a wallet or pack, take*
*it; and if you don't have a sword,*
*sell your robe to buy one.*
Luke 22:36

Your first line of defense against theft should be an in-home security system. You can get crazy and spend a lot of money, but if you're not hiding an extensive collection of precious jewels or sensitive government documents, you don't need a million dollar top-of-the-line safe.

You need to sit down and decide your needs and applications. How often do you expect someone to break into your home? Would they be able to set up camp and spend as long as they wanted going through your stuff? Would watchful neighbors alert the authorities, shortening their time in your home?

*The Constitution is not an instrument for the government to restrain the people. It is an instrument for the people to restrain the government—lest it come to dominate our lives and interests.*

*Patrick Henry*

What kind of stuff do you want to put in a safe? Are you trying to protect your gun collection, keep an emergency reserve of cash in the event your bank fails, or store wills and legal documents so they can be accessed at any time and not just when the banks are open?

In addition, laws are sometimes changed that make instant criminals of law-abiding citizens overnight. Many gun owners have found themselves in the tenuous position of having an illegal weapon due to the enactment of restrictive gun laws. It makes sense to have a secure place for these items while waiting to see if these laws are overturned.

ഓൻരു

The IRS has been known to obtain warrants to search the safe deposit boxes of those they are auditing. Innocent coin collections and cash can be looked at as an attempt to evade income taxes by these overzealous agents. Home security systems can keep snoopy IRS agents from getting the wrong impression about what your collections and cash reserves are really for.

How much you spend on a home safe should be in proportion to what you feel your possessions are worth. You may want to purchase extra insurance instead of a safe to cover those items that you don't want to take a financial loss on (but that don't hold special value to you). Old heirlooms that have a high dollar appraisal but no sentimental worth fall into this category.

Any gun collection should be considered well worth the financial investment to secure, especially those that don't have a paper trail leading to you. A secure place to store cash on hand, important documents, and things that prying eyes shouldn't have access to should be given high priority when calculating the cost benefits of a home safe.

## The Basics of Home Safety

If you are foolish enough to leave on vacation without stopping newspaper delivery, leaving the phone off the hook, or having the post office hold your mail, then expect to come back to a house that burglars have taken their time going through with a fine-toothed comb. Common sense measures are always your first priority in a safety system.

You want to make a thief's work harder by making him think you're either at home or will be returning home at any time. It's a mind game, and you have to play it effectively.

Look at your home through the eyes of a thief and try to imagine the things that would keep you from attempting a break-in. Keep lights on in a few rooms that have high visibility from outside. Keep the television or radio going, a little louder than usual. If you're away for an extended period, take the phone off the hook. All this activity gives the impression that someone is in the house.

Burglars are less likely to break into a house that is protected by a gun, especially if they're not quite sure if the owner is at home. A simple NRA decal in a conspicuous place like the window in an entryway door has been shown to be a deterrent to criminals.

Criminals "case a joint" before actually attempting to burglarize it. You want to make this as difficult for them as possible. The following recommendations will either make a burglar think twice about trying to break into your home or make it so difficult for him, he'll give up and leave.

- ✔ Replace outside lights with automatic motion-detecting ones that come on when someone passes through the beam of the photocell.

- ✔ Trim back shrubbery, trees, and plants from the house. Overgrowth creates a safe haven for the burglar, with hiding spots galore. Having prickly plants like cacti, holly bushes, or roses will also keep him from hiding too close to the house. (Just give yourself enough room from these plants to escape through a window in the event of a fire.)

- ✔ Running a bead of caulk around the edges of storm windows makes removing them quietly almost impossible. Double-paned windows are also harder for thieves to get through.

- ✔ There are safety issues involved in installing iron bars outside of bedroom windows, or in nailing or bolting them shut. These deterrents can easily cost the life of a family member in the event of a fire by blocking their escape from the house. It's far better to have a safety bar across the top of the lower pane to keep someone from being able to raise it from outside. This bar can easily and quickly be removed if a fire breaks out.

✔ Quality locks are another item in your deterrent system. If you have to skip the wallpaper in the bathroom and the designer paint job in the kitchen, always buy quality locks and hardware. Buy heavy duty striker plates and locks that are secured to the frame of the house and not just to the trim around the door.

✔ Dead bolts add an extra measure of protection. Building codes don't allow builders to install keyed dead bolts on the inside of a house for fire safety reasons. However, if you have a thumb-latch dead bolt underneath or near a window, a thief merely has to break the glass to reach in and turn the lock. You can replace it with a keyed lock, but you should hang a spare key near enough to the dead bolt (although out of reach of a thief on the other side of the door) that anyone can get out of the house if it catches on fire.

If you find yourself moving, always look for areas with low crime rates. Go to the local police station and find out which neighborhoods suffer from a higher amount of break-ins and avoid purchasing a home there if at all possible. Even if you have to commute a little farther to get to work, the peace of mind you have will be worth it.

## The Refuge Room

The refuge room is also known as a *panic room* or a *safe room*. The most important thing about this room is that it be in a location that you and your family can reach in a hurry. Since most burglaries occur at night, your refuge room should either be close to the bedroom or be the bedroom itself.

This room should have a door that can be locked from the inside. If your cell phone doesn't work well inside your house, then ideally you should have a separate phone line in this one room that isn't tied to the rest of the house. The outside line should be protected in metal conduit to make it harder for anyone to cut it.

The purpose of a refuge room is to keep the person who has broken into your house away from you and your family as long as possible. To that end, you're going to need to install a solid core door with heavy locks and the hinges on the inside. You're going to want this door to lock from the outside as well, since this is the room you'll be storing your valuables in.

Your refuge room is going to need more than a strong door. Any burglar whose brain isn't fried on dope will know that he can kick through a standard Sheetrock® wall and enter a room. Plywood paneling will add sturdiness and greater impenetrability to your refuge room walls. You don't even have to remove the drywall. Just nail the plywood in place over it. Mark your studs so that you're nailing into framing members and not just the drywall itself.

---

### Safe Room Supplies
### (from the U.S. Department of Justice)

Non-perishable foods
Bottled water
First-aid kit
Any maintenance medicines
Flashlight and extra batteries
Clothes
Sanitation supplies
Important documents
Blankets
Cash
Duct tape
Potassium-iodine tablets
(to prevent radiation sickness)

You will also want to keep your
guns and ammo
in this room

---

ഇൠ

Of course, if you're starting from scratch and planning your room before the house is constructed, or designing an addition to the house, then reinforced cement block walls is the preferred material for a refuge room.

## Inexpensive Gun Safes

If money is a concern, you can buy inexpensive safes or gun chests that, with a little bit of ingenuity, will give you some level of protection. If the total value of your weapons and assets that you want to store is less than $5000, then an inexpensive safe that is bolted down properly will deter most amateur burglars.

The drawback to an inexpensive safe is that the thickness of metal in the safe is less than adequate and the doors are not of sufficient construction to withstand an attack from anyone with a crowbar or an axe.

These safes are easy to move and place because they're not as heavy as some of their more expensive cousins. Many discount stores, warehouse clubs, and sporting goods stores carry these safes. They range in price from $900 to $1,500.

One thing about safes—if you don't bolt it to the floor (preferably a concrete floor), then even if you spend $10,000 on it, the safe won't afford you very much protection. A thief will simply roll it over and hack into it from the back, side, or top.

Try to position the safe inside a closet or closed-in space so that a burglar can't get much swinging room to wield an axe or crowbar when trying to break into it.

You can frame-in the safe with 2 x 4s and Sheetrock® or panel around it. Make sure that bolt holes are pre-drilled in the bottom of the safe so that you can secure it to the floor. If the model you're looking at doesn't have arrangements made for bolting it down, don't buy it.

The more weight that you can add to the gun safe, the better. You want to make it as hard as possible for the thief to move it around. To that end, store large amounts of ammunition in the bottom of your safe in addition to your guns and other valuables. However, avoid storing your gunpowder or primers in the safe. These items are volatile and can easily explode.

Homak and Liberty offer models that fit within this category and are reasonably priced. In addition, Liberty safes are also fireproof rated to withstand 1200 degree heat anywhere from 30 minutes to 2 ½ hours, depending on the model.

## High End Safes and Gun Vaults

Those wanting a higher level of security for their goods will want to invest in a gun vault. The foremost consideration is construction design. The most desirable would be a one-piece molded safe with no seams at all, but they don't make such a critter.

You will want a safe with as few seams as possible, and those seams should be solidly welded. Try to avoid those that are spot welded. Any break in the seam welds is a place for a thief to insert a crowbar to pry the metal up.

The price for this safe will be directly related to the thickness of the metal that it's constructed from, but still, ten gauge metal is about as thin as you want to go with your high-end safe.

The door construction is as important as the shell. Note the hinges—are they located inside or outside of the safe? Despite what the salesman may tell you, common sense says that inside the safe is better.

The door should have locking bolts on all four sides. Doors with locking bolts on less than four sides and that have the hinges compromised can be removed.  There are several options in locking mechanisms, and you should study up on these before making a choice on the model safe you buy.

Liberty, Browning, Fort Knox, and Smith Security Safes build not only high quality safes, but the doors and frames for constructed gun vaults. If you go with a gun vault, you can also design it to be your safe room as well.

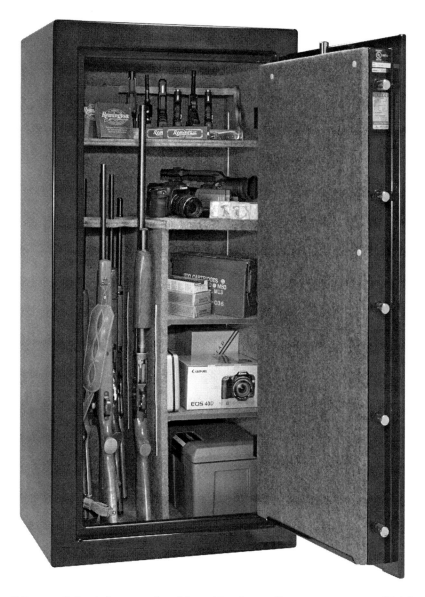

*Liberty Colonial gun safe with a 45 minute fire-rating at 1200°F. Units start at $1329. (Photo courtesy Liberty Safes. Used with permission.)*

*Liberty Presidential gun safe with a 2 1/2 hour fire-rating at 1200°F. Units start at $3699. (Photo courtesy Liberty Safes. Used with permission.)*

*Liberty walk-in vault door. Units start at $6259. (Photo courtesy Liberty Safes. Used with permission.)*

## What to Look For When Buying A Gun Safe

Make sure you do adequate research on different brands before buying your safe.

Things to take into consideration are:

1. The most security for your money. Compare fire and burglary ratings among the brands and models you are considering.

2. Buy a safe that fits your needs...and then some. Make a list of what you want to store and buy your safe a little bigger than needed so you can add as you see fit.

3. Make sure the interior is adequate. You'll need 58" minimum interior height to store long rifles. Look for shelves and compartments, and note if they are adjustable or not.

4. Choose a safe that you can easily use but has the best protection. Most homeowners opt for a safe bolted to the floor in a closet or a safe room.

5. If you're hiring someone to install your safe, ask these questions!

   - Are they bonded and insured?
   - How long have they been in business?
   - Do they have a service department?
   - Are they knowledgeable? Ask them to show you the difference between a burglar and fire safe. A fire safe is not necessarily burglar-proof and vice versa.

# CHAPTER 2
## SIMPLE HIDING PLACES

*Moreover, anyone who does not provide for his*
*people, especially for his family, has disowned the*
*faith and is worse than an unbeliever.*
1 Timothy 5:8

With the threats that we face today from our current economic crisis and with terrorist cells operating in most major cities, it makes sense to have more than a storage facility for those items that we may need in the event of a terrorist attack, civil unrest, or government collapse and anarchy.

Before you start prying up floorboards or cutting holes in your drywall, however, look at what you have and what you want to stash. Make a list of what goods you want to hide and who you want to hide them from. Governments act foolish in times of crisis, oftentimes placing their citizens in greater harm by confiscating weapons in an attempt to reign in rampaging mobs.

All this does is put the average law-abiding citizen in greater danger. We have a responsibility to our families and loved ones to protect them, regardless of government proscriptions.

Put yourself in the mind of a burglar, or a government agent, and look at your home. Where would be the first place a burglar would look for valuables? If you have a safe, it's probably his first stop, which kind of defeats its purpose. A lot of times the places that are right in front of your nose are the least obvious places that someone will notice when looking for a stash.

ℰℭ

## Putting Empty Space To Work

First, you will need to have a basic knowledge of construction and carpentry as we get further along. As we go through the various hiding places you may have available, from the more simple to the more complex, you will also need to be familiar with the use of common tools – drills, saws, levels, etc. If you aren't handy with these things, there are books available from your local building supply store or library that can help you.

Don't just go in and rip out a spot in your house. Carefully plan and execute your various hides. Do a professional job in building or remodeling your hide's location. One hide done well is worth ten done sloppily.

You have empty pockets of space all around you in your house. There is empty space inside furniture, light fixtures, cabinets, curtain rods, walls, under stairwells, inside unused books, in attic spaces, in duct work – are you starting to get the picture? All these places can be utilized for hides.

Modern sofas and chairs can be upended, the staples removed from the fabric, and easily fit with hidden pockets on the inside. An Arrow™ staple gun from your local hardware store is all you need to reattach the fabric. Do a neat job that is undetectable from the original fastenings.

While you're in there, you can cut out cavities in the foam padding and put valuables there. Just be sure to replace enough

padding over the goods to give the correct feel if that area of the furniture is searched thoroughly.

The legs of wooden furniture like chairs or coffee tables can be drilled out, and the resultant cavity used as a hide. Your dining room table may be able to be fitted on the underneath side with a shallow false bottom that can be used to store a long rifle or shotgun.

While stereo speakers and televisions may make good hiding places, these are the items that thieves steal first. They may not be the best places to put jewelry or other valuables. Look for hiding places in things that cannot be easily toted off or removed.

If you think that humongous 72" television can't be taken, think again. I came home one day to find my back door smashed in, and my carpet and linoleum torn to shreds where thieves had drug my big 61" projection television across the floor and out the door. Burglars can be pretty determined. (If only they'd put that determination to good use!)

A hollowed out book in a library full of books can be a pretty effective hide. Use no more than the middle third of the book for the hide and secure the stash to the pages since one common way of seeing if books contain secret storage is to upend them and shake. If the thought of defacing a book makes you cringe, there are fake books available commercially that are hollowed out from the factory.

The empty cavity of a curtain rod is another place to store smaller items, as is your refrigerator. You

☙❧

can put credit cards inside of food packages and freeze them, unless food shortages make this a burglar's first take. Hiding your credit cards is advisable in case your house is broken into, but still keeps them accessible in the event of an emergency.

The hollow spaces behind kickplates on cabinets are also great places to store stuff. Gently pry them from the cabinet and replace as carefully.

The drawers in a module can all be shortened, and an access point made on the side. You can hide larger objects behind the drawers.

If the floors in your house are wooden floor joists over a basement or a crawl space, you can utilize the space in between the joists. Because the floor joists are part of the structural integrity of your home, under no circumstance should you cut these joists unless you have construction experience and know where to cut and how to reinforce the span.

U.S, Navy photo by Senior Chief Photographer's Mate Douglas E. Waite
[Public domain]

If your floor joists are also part of the ceiling structure of a downstairs room, the upperside of the drywall that comprises the ceiling of the downstairs room will be visible. These sheets are held in place not only with screws, but by abutting sheets of drywall. They are not structurally capable of holding a great deal of weight. Keep that in mind when deciding what to put in this space.

Interior wooden doors are usually hollow core. With a few simple tools the top and bottom can be cut out and the inside space used for storage.

ဆာ

*The interior of a hollow core door.*

Some doors have a fiberboard reinforcement on the inside, but this can easily be cut away and a cavity made.

The insulation in the attic space can be used as a hide. Be sure to wear long sleeves and gloves when handling fiberglass insulation. You can slice fiberglass batt insulation through the center and place items in between the layers.

Loose fill insulation can be raked back and then replaced when you've placed your stash. When moving this insulation around, be sure you don't block any eave or soffit vents. Also be careful that you don't step off the floor joists and fall through the ceiling.

Use picture frames that hold pictures of the family or diplomas to safely hide documents or cash. Any framed object that has no value except to the family will do. Don't keep all your cash or documents in frames however. Different types of hides are better so that if a burglar runs across one of your hides, he won't necessarily be able to find all of them.

Hides have been in use since ancient times. A book by Allen Fea titled *Secret Chambers and Hiding Spaces* is a look at older castles and mansions and the different hiding spaces and cubby holes incorporated into them. It's an interesting book for history or trivia buffs, and might even give you an idea or two about building hides in your home.

For instance, the following drawings show a cabinet with a fake back that could be used for storing any number of valuables.

ΣΟΣΒ

For those readers interested in reading this book, it can be obtained free from the Gutenberg Project as an eBook download. That website is www.gutenberg.org.

ଈଔ

# CHAPTER

## ELABORATE HIDES

*Be strong and of a good courage, fear not,*
*nor be afraid of them.*
Deuteronomy 31:6

Elaborate hides are those that utilize a little more creative and imaginative places to store your goods. Look at your house, at areas of wasted space, areas behind walls, above ceilings, and in the floor. There is literally a wealth of space within these areas that can be utilized for caches and stores. Remember, you're not just thinking in terms of guns. Anything of any value should be stored in such a manner that thieves and even rogue government agencies will be hard-pressed to find them.

## Modifying Floor, Ceiling, and Wall Systems

When you're trying to determine where to make modifications in your home, you must remember that the floor and ceiling joists are an integral part of the structural integrity of your home. You cannot just cut and route any way that you want. The same is true with load and non-load bearing walls.

Don't just assume that you know which walls and floors joists are supporting weight. If you have a basement or crawl space, go underneath the house and verify you can make the modifications you want. In the same vein, crawl into the attic space and make sure you're not going to cut into a board that is supporting a hallway and three walls.

The diagrams and charts on the next page will help you when you begin remodeling.

ഇരുട

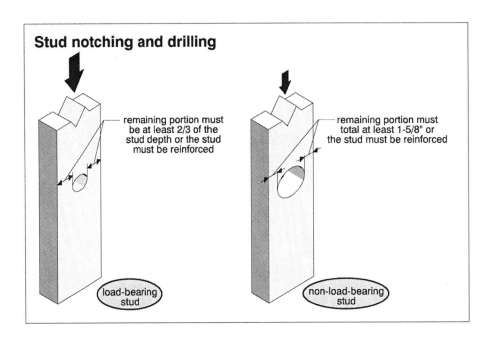

### Stud notching and drilling

remaining portion must be at least 2/3 of the stud depth or the stud must be reinforced

load-bearing stud

remaining portion must total at least 1-5/8" or the stud must be reinforced

non-load-bearing stud

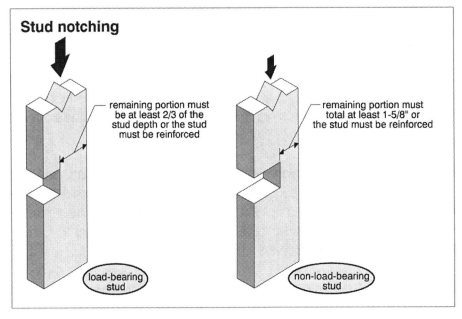

### Stud notching

remaining portion must be at least 2/3 of the stud depth or the stud must be reinforced

load-bearing stud

remaining portion must total at least 1-5/8" or the stud must be reinforced

non-load-bearing stud

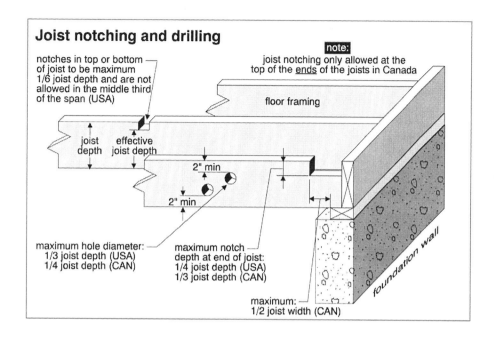

| Maximum Hole Sizes for Load Bearing Studs | |
|---|---|
| 2 x 4 | 1 3/8 inch |
| 2 x 6 | 2 3/16 inch |
| Maximum Hole Sizes in Non-load Bearing Studs | |
| 2 x 4 | 2 inches |
| 2 x 6 | 3 1/4 inches |
| Maximum hole sizes in Floor & Ceiling Joists | |
| 2 x 6 | 1 1/2 inches |
| 2 x 8 | 2 3/8 inches |
| 2 x 10 | 3 1/8 inches |
| 2 x 12 | 3 1/2 inches |

It's very important that you adhere to these guidelines. You don't want to compromise the structural integrity of your home.

You can take advantage of the space around a stairwell with a cleverly concealed entryway door that looks like a bookcase. The area under a stairwell that is usually reserved for a small closet still has plenty of dead space you can take advantage of. And let's not forget the stairs themselves. There are many ways to get creative with those.

You can design a drop ceiling into a room, and use the dead space there as a place to hide things. Look at the picture to the left and let your imagination run wild.

## Additional Choices for Hides

Do you have a basement? Is your house built on a crawl space? If so, you can design dummy drain and vent pipes into your existing plumbing to use as hides. Even if your house is built on a slab, you can design and bury what will appear as a cleanout or two around the house. Just make sure that it fits in logically with landscaping and that it doesn't look out of place. Don't

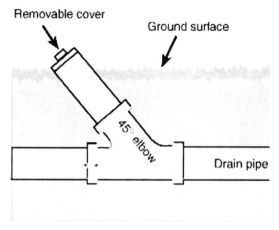

Removable cover

Ground surface

45° elbow

Drain pipe

have the pipe sticking out too far from the dirt. The sun will deteriorate PVC pipe.

Are you a master gardener with a steaming compost pile in your back yard? This is also an excellent location for a hide. Most people don't want to stick their hands in a rotting, smelly compost pile.

Encase your stash in a section of capped PVC pipe and bury it under the compost heap, preferably a foot or two into the ground. While this is a short-term stash and not a true cache, you'll still want to generously oil your weapon and wrap it in several layers of cloth.

You can also utilize an outdoor gutter drain for a hide. Simply lift the lid, attach your stash to the side and close it back up. Most thieves are strictly intent on what's inside your house, not what might be stored in the ground outside.

Any kind of storm drainage system can be used this way.

## Know Your Limitations

What started the American Revolution? Was it the taxation policies of the Crown? Was it England's arbitrary decision-making policies without the

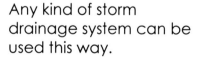

colonials' input? While all of these contributed to the frustrated feelings of the colonists, it was the British attempt to disarm the colonials at Lexington that started our American revolution.

The Founders of this country, blessed with wisdom from Almighty God, recognized that an armed citizenry was a free citizenry, and so designed a Constitution that would insure the right for all future generations of Americans to keep and bear arms.

> *Guard with jealous attention the public liberty.*
> *~Patrick Henry~*

We were given the blessing of governing ourselves, through a republic with duly elected representatives. But like any man-made creation, our government has fallen prey to a special brand of elitism that belongs strictly to those in power. They voice their disdain for the common man and do not attempt to hide their belief that the Second Amendment is an item of law never intended for the regular citizens of this country.

Knowing that our leaders keep trying unceasingly to limit or ban the availability of firearms should give you pause. If they do come to confiscate all weapons, our homes and our stashes, no matter how well planned and laid out, will not be able to be hidden for long. These stashes will hinder the common thief, but not a government intent on control.

But, if resistance was futile, Afghanistan would not be the quagmire in our war on terror that it is today. History is replete with examples of small pockets of resistance holding off a superior army. In no way am I advocating armed rebellion. All efforts to keep our fundamental rights should be engaged at the government level, through the courts and through the election of like-minded representatives.

However, if history has taught us anything, it's that all kingdoms fall. They may rise up again in a different incarnation, but all things come to an end. With today's technologies in metal detection and thermal imaging, should our government decide to confiscate our weapons, it wouldn't take long or be hard for them to do so.

෴

To that extent, weapons caching is a viable alternative to handing over your weapons.

# CHAPTER 4
## WEAPONS CACHING

*A well regulated militia being necessary to the security of a free State,*
*the right of the People to keep and bear arms shall not*
*be infringed.*
Second Amendment, U.S. Constitution

**D**espite our right to keep and bear arms as guaranteed by the Second Amendment to the Constitution, our government, from its inception, has attempted to enact some form of gun control aimed at maintaining a tight rein on particular groups of people.

Of course before the Revolutionary War, it was the British attempt to confiscate weapons that led to the colonials' demands for independence.

After our republic was formed, gun laws were enacted for black slaves and freedmen so that they couldn't rise up against the slave owners. After the Civil War, gun laws were rewritten during Reconstruction to again limit blacks and poor whites from owning weapons.

Today our government targets the entire civilian population with gun laws. These laws are no respecter of race, religion, or gender. It may very well come to a point in the future that the average gun owner is going to have to decide whether or not to turn over his weapons to the authorities when they come knocking on his door.

It's all very well and romantic sounding to say that they'll get your guns when they pry them from your cold dead hands, but in reality we have been trained to obey authority figures and going out in a blazing gun battle is not something that most of us will do. The sad but unfortunate fact is that we've gotten quite lazy, dependent on the courts to interpret our Constitution for us and on our government to provide for our needs.

ॐ

You do need to understand one thing—if you are seriously considering caching your weapons, you're not doing it so that one fine spring morning you can unearth your shotgun and go turkey hunting. You aren't burying these guns to dig up later to go skeet shooting or for target practicing.

You are storing against a future day when government breaks down because of terrorism or war. You are preparing for a day when calamity makes it necessary for you to protect yourself and your family against gangs and thugs intent on anarchy.

You will be burying your weapons so that one day either you or future generations can rise up against a tyrannical government and resist, by force of arms if necessary.

You should carefully consider your course in this matter. Today, while you still can, you should use every legal means to insure your constitutional rights for you and your children. You should not allow apathy to steal those freedoms that have been endowed by God.

It is said that we are given the government that we deserve. If we want this republic to continue, then we are going to have to be bothered to be the constant defenders of our liberties, ever diligent to safeguard that which our ancestors spilled so much blood to establish, and guarding jealously what our husbands and wives, fathers and mothers, and our sons and daughters die to defend to this day.

> *Teach the children quietly, for some day sons and daughters,*
> *will rise up and fight while we stood still.*
>
> *Can you hear me, can you hear me running?*
> *Can you hear me running,*
> *can you hear me calling you?*
>
> *~from the song "Silent Running"*
> *by Mike and the Mechanics*

ഇയ

## Hides vs. Caches

It's important that you understand that there is a difference between a hide and a cache. The hide is meant to secure your valuables from an unwanted intrusion but still keep them handily available. A cache is a long term storage device for goods that you may or may not need months or years down the road. A cache is not meant to be accessed unless it's an emergency.

Weapons caching has been one of the strategies used successfully in two of the major wars fought in this century. If you are serious about surviving in a war-time environment, then you should study the tactics of the Viet Cong. They were able to withstand the armies of two countries that had superior arms and fire power, and their victory was due in a large part to their ability to set up elaborate weapons caches.

Guns and ammunition were woven into the thatch of the huts that the Viet Cong villagers lived in. Guns were found in rice granaries and ammunition in bamboo poles. Arms and explosives were found under smoldering cooking fires, and in tunnels dug under the huts.

The Viet Cong not only utilized their environment, they utilized weapons that had been lost at sea. Coastal freighters sunk by the Japanese during WWII were a gold mine of arms, ammunition, and explosives. Patient Viet Cong divers salvaged tons of armaments from as far down as

sixty feet without the use of air tanks and as far down as ninety feet with the use of a simple air hose.

Cemeteries were also a favorite place for the Viet Cong to place a cache. Ground observers believe that by 1968 most of the arms smuggled into the cities were by way of coffins. The Viet Cong were imaginative and industrious, taking advantage of not only their surroundings, but their resources as well.

You need to also look at your surroundings and resources to get the best feel of what can and cannot be accomplished.

## Caching Strategies

As you plan your caching strategies, you need to look at locations with the following in mind:

- Positions for lookouts
- Landmark identification and placement
- Accessibility
- Concealment
- Escape routes

You will not be burying anything in your own backyard. You are going to scout country roads, garbage dumps, abandoned buildings, caverns, ponds ... you get the picture. You want these weapons as far away from you as possible without losing them. Septic tanks and sewers are really not ideal places to store a cache any more. In drug raids conducted today, if there is a septic tank on the premises, it's the first place the authorities look. Garbage cans, garbage bins, and wastebaskets are also first on the list of places that authorities search when looking for what they consider "contraband" weapons.

ଛେଠଔ

Ideally your cache site should have surroundings where you can place lookouts to watch for uninvited guests while you're concealing or digging up your cache. However, with modern night vision scopes and thermal imaging techniques, a lookout is superfluous if you're trying to evade the authorities. If they've got you on their radar, the likelihood of a lookout forewarning you is pretty slim.

As few people as possible should know about your cache. Fewer still should even be able to guess where it's remotely located. You're going to have to stifle the impulse to brag to your fellow gun buddies about what you're doing. Loose lips sink ships.

You need to put your cache in a place where you can use identifying landmarks as well as a GPS system and a compass to locate it. This is a very important step. Your cache is no good if you can't find it.

Your cache should be accessible without having to bypass security measures or without you having to explain to a ton of passersby what you're doing digging in that flower bed with a 10 foot auger.

Concealment is another factor you should be planning out. You should take pictures of your cache site BEFORE you start the hiding process so that you can return it to the condition it was in before you started. A well-thought out plan that is executed with perfection will be more successful than a plan that's flying by bootstraps and a prayer.

Your cache site should also allow you more than one escape route in case your position is compromised. Don't ever put yourself in the position of being cornered. Your cache site should be able to include several dummy sites where you can place misleading trails that will hopefully throw any tracker or snoop off the scent of your real cache.

## Urban Caching Challenges

Those who live in the city face caching challenges that are unique. Their rural caching cousins have many more choices in available sites. While not impossible to accomplish, you're going to have to be that much more inventive and prepared with your cache sites.

Abandoned buildings are one prospect. You can find a dark, quiet corner where you can remove some blocks or tile to create an improvised vault. Remember, if the place is nasty enough (you're going to have to get over your own revulsion) most people will avoid it like the plague.

As with a rural cache, it's best not to put all your eggs in one basket. Spread your cache over several areas so that if one is discovered by accident you still have access to the rest of your stuff. Again, the threat of discovery is why it's best to put weapons that can't be traced to you in your cache.

෨෬

# CHAPTER
# PREPARING A CACHE

*No kingdom can be secured otherwise than by arming the
people. The possession of arms is the distinction
between a freeman and a slave.*
James Burgh, 1774

You're going to need to prepare your cache carefully and with
forethought. You'll need to determine the contents, the materials, and
the assembly of your caches. There are four classes of items that can be
considered for a cache:

✔ **Prohibited items** - things like weapons, forged I.D., silencers, etc.

✔ **Items that may become unattainable in the event of a complete
economic breakdown** - things like bullets, reloading equipment,
smokeless powder, hand tools, medicines, foodstuffs, candles, radios,
etc.

✔ **Items that need to remain a secret** - like information on the various
caches you have, documents that can be used to find you, etc.

✔ **Items that can be easily hidden or stolen** - gold, silver, money, family
heirlooms, address books, etc. Anything up to 50 pounds qualifies
here if you deem it valuable.

Try to think about what you will need if the nearest store is miles away and
you have no power. Now go through your lists and determine which of
those items really needs to be cached in long-term storage or if they can
be hidden above ground or stored regularly.

After you've compiled your lists, go through each item and mark it with an
"S" for storage, "H" for hide, and "C" for cache. Decide which of your items

∞○∞

will be needed on short notice (like guns, ammunition, information about other caches, shovels and so forth.)

Group your items for similar needs—for example, keep your bullets, primers and reloading equipment in the same cache (although your primers will need to be separated from your black powder to prevent a possible explosion in your cache).

Try to distribute the weight and size of your items amongst all your caches. Once you've grouped everything together, count up the number of caches, how you're going to store them, and the types of containers and storage containers you're going to need.

Now is the time to decide whether you want to go through with this or not. Once you've shelled out the money for the materials needed, it'd be wasteful to not follow through with your plan.

It's best to make up smaller caches spread over a wider area. You don't want to concentrate all your valuables in one place. Try to get a good balance here—you're not a human backhoe and you're going to have to take your physical limitations into account.

There are various levels of caches and your needs will determine which you employ. However, having both of them is necessary if you're truly preparing for a day that you might need to hide or can no longer go back home.

৪৩৫৫

The **survival cache** is meant to assist you if you've been cut off from your main source of supplies and you need something until you can get back to it. This cache will have a couple of day's worth of immediate-need items like foodstuffs, a military first-aid kit, and a weapon with a few day's worth of ammunition.

The **E & E cache (Escape and Evasion)** will have a complete getaway kit in addition to a pistol or folding-stock rifle and ammunition. The E & E cache is meant to be well hidden but able to be grabbed up at a moment's notice. You'll have stuff to treat injuries in this cache, as well as items to use to change your appearance, such as scissors and hair dye, water purifications tablets, and MREs. Including several hundred dollars worth of cash in here would be prudent—in 10 and 20 dollar denominations.

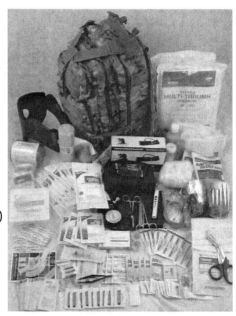

Everything in this kit should fit into a small backpack with the exception of the rifle. You can buy a hair coloring kit at Walmart, but you'll be best served to get your first-aid kit from a military surplus store. These kits contain more usable items for true survival measures.

## Different Packs for Your Survival Cache

You'll need different types of packs to store in a cache. You are more familiar with your own needs and may want to change up some of the suggested items on the following pages or make your own unique packs.

Military surplus stores and web sites have the medic surgical instrument kits and the QuikClot First Response™ sponges. Survivalist, along with hiking and camping resources, can also hook you up with other first-aid supplies you may want to store. Most prescription medications have a limited shelf life, so maintenance medications should probably not be cached long-term. You may want to include vacuum-sealed pouches of multi-vitamins, B-complex vitamins, C vitamins, and zinc. These are the most effective when dealing with mild colds and a lack of adequate nutrition. Vacuum sealing them will keep the oxygen level down and deterioration of the pills at bay.

In addition to these packs, you can also design packs for tools, defense, communication equipment, and items for bartering.

## The Medical Pack

| | |
|---|---|
| Band-Aids | Eye Wash |
| Compress Gauze Bandages | Antibiotic Eye Ointment |
| Petroleum Gauze Bandages | Rubbing Alcohol |
| Elastic Bandages | Clean cotton rags, absorbent |
| Tape | Cotton swabs, long-stemmed |
| Antibiotic Ointment | Ipecac Syrup |
| Ammonia Inhalant | Soap |
| Povidone Iodine Solution | Sterile Water |
| Latex Gloves | Blood Pressure Cuff |
| Anaphylactic Shock Kit | Pain Pills |
| Various Sutures, with Needles | Military Medic Surgical Instrument Kit |
| Scalpels | Quickclot First Response™ |
| Splints | Vacuum-sealed packs of vitamins |
| Aloe Vera Gel | Aspirin |
| | |

## The Travel Pack

| | |
|---|---|
| 1 quart of water | 2 flashlights |
| Collapsible 5-gallon water jug | Extra batteries for flashlights |
| Water purification tablets | Rechargeable flashlight with car charger |
| Energy bars | Soap |
| MREs for one week | Pocket Knife |
| Several changes of clothes | Bleach |
| 2 waterproof tarps | Insect repellent |
| Thermal blanket | 2 pulleys |
| Sleeping bag | 100 ft. of 1/2" diameter Goldline rope |
| Coat | Magnifying glass |
| Matches | Toilet paper |
| Compass | Signaling mirror |
| Maps | Pistols |
| Retractable fishing rod and kit | 500 rounds of ammunition for pistols |

## Pipe Cache Materials

Because of the advances in technologies today, the cacher has a much larger array of materials to choose from than in previous generations. The burial containers must take three things into account, however:

- Must be impervious to moisture or water
- Must be able to resist the crushing forces of dirt
- Must be resealable

The last item is pretty important because you may need to access your cache in an emergency and being able to reseal it will be necessary.

ഇൻൽ

Since most caches are put into the ground in a vertical position, it's best to use standard plastic plumbing pipe or PVC. It's also know as DWV pipe - Drain, Waste, Vent pipe.

There are several types of DWV pipe. 4-inch pipe and under comes in a thin-walled type and a thicker wall called Schedule 40. 6-inch diameter pipe and above comes in Schedule 40 and Schedule 80. Schedule 40 pipe is what you will want to use for your cache material. Schedule 80 is very expensive and there's no appreciable benefit to using it. Schedule 40 pipe is more than adequate for your needs.

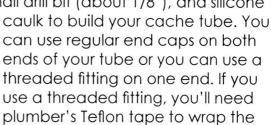

In addition to your pipe material, you'll need end caps, PVC primer, PVC glue, common lube grease, a small drill bit (about 1/8"), and silicone caulk to build your cache tube. You can use regular end caps on both ends of your tube or you can use a threaded fitting on one end. If you use a threaded fitting, you'll need plumber's Teflon tape to wrap the

threads of the male end cap. A 4-inch diameter pipe will hold ammunition and magazines. A minimum 6-inch diameter pipe is needed for guns, and while 8 inches is better, it's also more expensive.

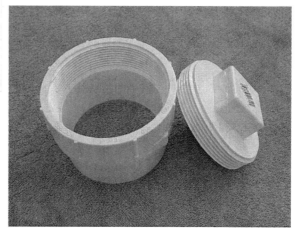

The 8-inch pipe is twice the cost per foot of 6-inch pipe, as are the fittings that go on it. Adapters and screw-in plugs for the 6-inch pipe are common, but are not available for the 8-inch pipe.  End caps run about $15.00 each for the 6-inch pipe, whereas the 8-inch endcaps will run you around $40.00 apiece. It ultimately depends on the size cache you want to build.

For instance, a 60-inch section of 8-inch pipe will hold two full-sized rifles, four assault rifles, four or five pistols, dozens of magazines, and loads of ammunition. A 60-inch length insures that even the longest semi-auto weapon will fit in the tube, and that the cache contents will settle to the bottom further away from a possible scan from a metal detector.

## Building Your Cache Tube

You will take one of your slip-on end caps and glue it to one end of the tube. Prime the outer surface of the pipe and the inner surface of the cap. The primer removes dirt and grease, and softens the plastic to prepare it for gluing.

Allow the primer to dry and then coat both surfaces generously with PVC glue. PVC glue melts the plastic so that when the two surfaces join, they actually weld together once the glue has evaporated.

With one continuous motion push and twist, turning the cap into place on the pipe, and hold. This twisting motion makes sure that all surfaces of the pipe and cap are well-coated with glue, removes air bubbles, and insures a bond. Hold the cap in place for about 15 seconds.  This is the bottom end of the cache tube.

Do not use a fast-set glue when gluing the components of your tube together. You need time to make sure that the caps and/or adapters are in place before the bonding process is complete.

What fitting you put on the top end of your cache tube depends on how you want to access your cache. If you want to unscrew a plug end, then you'll need to glue the female adapter to the top end. Before you glue

ဢၧ

your adapter to the tube, be sure to remove the plug. You don't want to get any primer or glue on the threads. Once you have your cache filled, you'll cover the threads with Teflon tape before sealing.

If you're building an 8-inch cache or just want to use a slip on end cap for your 6-inch tube, then be prepared to drill about a 1/8 inch hole in the end of your second end cap. When you put a solid end cap on the other end of your tube, you're going to be compressing whatever air is in the pipe. Sometimes this air pressure will equalize, and sometimes it won't. The cap is going to want to come off. The only way to avoid that is to drill a vent hole in the top of the cap that you will fill with silicone caulk before burying the tube. However, don't drill a vent hole unless it's absolutely necessary.

## Building A Bucket Cache

Generally a cache is prepared with a focus on the time frame the items will be in the ground. Pipe caches can last indefinitely. The bucket cache is designed to last three to five years.

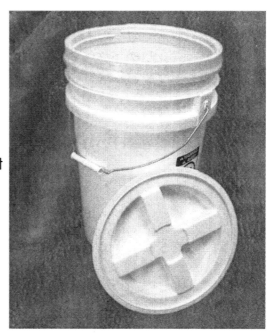

The bucket cache is fairly simple and easy to make. This stash won't contain more stuff than a person could carry if needed, as it's mainly to provide enough minimal comfort for a person to stay in one place for a few nights. You'd be able to get clean, eat a few good meals, have clean water, and get a decent night's sleep.

The bucket cache should have enough packed in it will keep a person going for a few days without the need to resupply. These caches are good to plant along an escape route that you would devise to get you out of an area after a natural disaster, civil unrest, a terrorist attack, or the breakdown of government.

You should assume that you would have already packed a bag with some extra clothes and hopefully brought along a blanket or sleeping bag. Each cache along your escape route should provide you with essential tools and survival items that you'll need to make it.

Of course the first thing you're going to start off with is the **bucket**. You'll need to get a gasketed lid, one with an O-ring seal to make it air-tight. They also make a two-piece screw-in lid that's called a Gamma Seal™ like the ones pictured below. The outer ring snaps onto the bucket like a regular lid, and the inner ring screws in.

The bucket has many uses, not the least of which is holding all the contents of your cache. However, once you unearth it, the bucket can be used to

haul water, used as a wash basin, or even used as a toilet.

It can be used to gather food like berries, mushrooms, or other edible items that you forage. It can be used to keep food from the reach of hungry animals. Fresh meat placed in the bucket and then secured in a running stream is considered a primitive but acceptable refrigeration system.

You'll want a **poncho** in your cache items. A standard military poncho has bungee cords attached to the corners so that you can use it for a makeshift shelter if the need arises. It's also useful in bad weather.

You'll want at least one **knife** in your kit. You should have a pocket knife with you at all times, but at least one skinning knife should be packed in your cache. Remember, this is a survival cache—most likely you'll be

෧෬

hunting for a significant amount of your food and you need a way to prepare it.

I would also recommend some kind of **knife sharpening kit—** either a small Lansky™ kit or a plain stone. You'll want to keep your knife blades honed at all times so that you're always prepared in a hunting or self-protection sense.

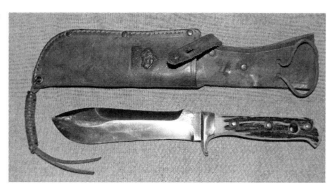

Pack a **flashlight** of some sort. A Mini-Maglite® is a good light, and you can buy one with LED lights now. They may be a little more expensive on the front end, but they're durable and will withstand harsh conditions. Be sure to pack **extra batteries** for whatever flashlight or other equipment you pack.

Don't take any chances that water will be readily available. Pack about a half-dozen bottles of bottled water. Also pack **water purification tablets** so that you can make use of any water supply you run across.

**Toilet paper** should be a staple in each cache that you plant along your proposed escape route. There's nothing more miserable than trying to "clean up" with only the elements of nature at your disposal.

Along with your personal hygiene supplies, don't forget to pack **soap** and a **toothbrush.** It seems so simple and the one item that wouldn't be neglected, but you'd be surprised how many people leave out these items. Bar soap is recommended and preferably, one like the old-time lye soaps that are still available. You'll be able to use this soap as a shampoo alternative without gunking your hair up with chemicals. Don't forget some antiperspirant as well.

You're going to want to have **MREs** (meals, ready-to-eat) packed in your cache. MREs are mini-survival kits all in themselves. You can purchase them at military surplus outlets, and there are also scads of web sites that you can order them from.

While hopefully you grabbed several changes of clothes on your way out, you should also pack a few changes of **underclothes**. It would also be good to have a **washcloth** or two in your cache. Nothing is more morale-busting than dirty underwear and a sweaty, stinky body.

Other items that you may find useful in a bucket cache would be a **drinking cup, eating utensils, gloves, string or rope**, and of course a **first-aid kit.**

And of course last, but not least, you may want to pack a **pistol and ammunition** if you'll be unable to get to one of your weapons caches in a reasonable time. A bucket is not the ideal firearms cache container, but you can make it work.

You'll want to clean and oil your pistol well. Try to avoid Cosmoline in this situation. Cleaning the Cosmoline off a pistol in primitive conditions will be challenging to say the least. Use a good lube oil.

Pack the pistol and ammunition separately from each other. The oil from the pistol can break down the primers in the ammunition, and then your ammo is worthless.

You can build a small cache tube for the ammunition that will fit in the bucket or use heavy plastic bags. If you use plastic bags, it would be good to use a vacuum sealer to close them.

Packing the bucket is simple. Make sure the bucket is clean and seals well. If the lid doesn't have an O-ring seal, you can use silicone caulk as a last resort... but you'll have a heck of a time trying to get the lid off when you finally retrieve your cache.

Put the water bottles on the bottom so that if they leak, they won't get everything else wet. Then pack everything else into the bucket and place

℘○℘

a desiccant packet (silicone gel) on top to absorb any moisture than might condensate inside the bucket while buried.

| Your Bucket List | |
|---|---|
| Bucket | Gamma Lid or lid with O'ring seal |
| Poncho | Knife |
| Flashlight | Knife-sharpening kit |
| Extra batteries | Toilet paper |
| Water | Soap |
| Water purification tablets | Toothbrush and toothpaste |
| MREs | Underclothes |
| Washcloths | Gloves |
| Drinking cup | String or rope |
| Eating utensils | First-aid kit |
| Pistol | Ammunition |

## Preparing and Packing Your Weapons Cache

Once you have your cache tube built, you'll want to prepare your weapons for storage. Try to pick weapons that have little wood or have a synthetic stock. Military-type weapons have little wood that will deteriorate and hence, store well.

The first thing you'll want to do is clean and grease your weapons well. While many people swear by Cosmoline as the grease of choice to cache weapons, cleaning it off the weapon in primitive conditions is again challenging and not necessary. There are many types of lithium-based oils with rust-inhibitors that can be used to oil down your weapon. Many companies manufacture a cotton picker spindle grease that is almost liquid at room temperature that's excellent for this application. You can check with a farm equipment dealership or order it on the Internet.

ଐଚ୍ଛ

You can wrap you weapons in a plastic sleeve for additional protection. You can buy rolls of plastic sleeving material that are 10 or 12 inches wide, 3 to 4 mil thick. While it would be great if you have the means to vacuum seal these sleeves, it's not necessary.

Another material you can wrap your guns in is VCI paper (Volatile and Vapor Corrosion Inhibiting Paper). It's the same paper that is used to wrap automotive parts and that the military uses for storage of metal items. It is impregnated with chemicals to prevent corrosion and rust. Suppliers for this and other items mentioned in this book are listed in the back in the resource section.

You should build a smaller cache tube for your ammunition and place it in the larger tube. This will keep your ammunition separate from any contact with grease that might destroy your primers.

You need to be careful to not get grease in your laser or telescopic sights. The same goes for your scope. It's not recommended that you remove your scope for storing your weapon because it may be impossible for you to re-zero it in later on. However, if you're going to remove the scopes from your weapons for storage, build a cache tube for those as well and store it in the same larger cache tube. Try not to disassemble your weapon any more than that. It's easy to lose parts and then your weapon will be useless. Even more importantly, don't store the parts from one gun in separate caches. If one cache is discovered and lost, your gun parts in the other cache tube are just junk metal.

You may want to make a wooden disc the same diameter as the cache tube, with a long dowel rod that is placed in the bottom of the cache tube. Since cache tubes may be difficult at best (or impossible at worst) to dig up, this would insure that any small item in the tube could be raised and retrieved.

Pack your cache tube. Use at least two ounces of silica gel in a 60-inch tube to absorb any moisture. While there are other desiccants out there, be sure to steer clear of any that have a salt content (like calcium chloride for example). These chemicals are highly corrosive to metal.

Generously grease the section of tube the end cap will sit on. Grease your end cap generously as well and twist it into place. If the cap will not stay on, drill a small hole in the top to relieve the air pressure and then seal with silicone caulk.

If you're using a threaded cap, wrap the threads with Teflon tape and then screw in tightly, making sure the tube is sealed well.

If your cache tube will be buried for a very long period of time (10-30 years) glue your cap in place. The same goes if your cache site is in a hostile environment such as underwater or in a swamp.

Don't load your cache tube with more weight than you can pick up since once you've selected your site and have prepared it for the cache, you'll have to tote it to the hole to place it. Under no circumstances should you load your cache tube at the site. That's just asking for trouble and discovery.

# CHAPTER 6
## CONCEALING A CACHE

*Before a standing army can rule,*
*the people must be disarmed.*
Noah Webster

You've got your supplies and weapons all lined up, your cache tubes or buckets are prepared, and you're ready to find a place to bury them. How do you start?

First you need to look at your surroundings and expand outward. If you live in the city in an apartment, you might be able to utilize a flower bed in the complex to place an emergency hide. For those of you who are rural dwellers, a place in some nearby woods may be where you want to conceal your first of several travel packs.

Three main points to consider when scoping for a location to bury a weapons or E & E (Escape and Evasion) cache is:

- Landmarks
- Accessibility
- Security

Instead of hoofing it, checking out cache sites by sight alone, get a copy of the latest topographical map from your state or the federal Department of the Interior that covers a 30-40 mile radius of your surrounding area.

Learn to become familiar with orienting yourself with a map and compass. The military has reprint manuals that will help you. Amazon.com is also another resource for additional books on the subject.

Practice your map reading and compass exercises BEFORE you head out

☙C13

to the deep woods or get stuck in the boonies. Most of the time these areas are remote enough that cell phone coverage is spotty.

Plat maps from the tax assessor's office are also useful in showing land 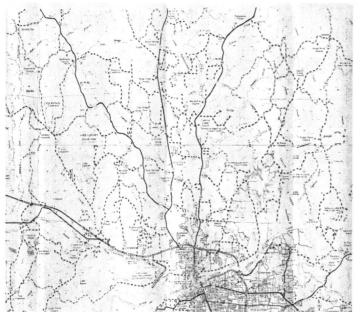 ownership and surveying landmarks for the area you're interested in for storing your cache.

Look for forest or wilderness areas under private ownership, rocky or mountainous terrain, land adjoining swampland, or state and federal recreation areas that afford a little privacy. Pick three or four areas that you could possibly work in as unobserved as possible.

## Landmarks

When considering where to put a stash, the hardest element to contend with are landmarks. All humans need some type of landmark to orient themselves to their surroundings. Treasure hunters have learned this lesson well, and focus their efforts on areas within the vicinity of old fence rows, old tree trunks, gazebos, old wells, lawn ornaments, old farmhouses, and the crumbling remains of chimneys.

You're beginning to get the picture. This narrows your secure cache sites considerably. A police search may look for a cache on every acre of land you own but not two farmhouses down. However, if you've buried it ten paces over from an old unique tree trunk in a national park, a treasure hunter will have a field day. Obvious, single, or human-made landmarks should be avoided.

## Accessibility

Using your topographical and/or plat maps, find areas that have access by little used country roads. You're going to want to stay within 30-40 miles of your home, but at least 10 miles out from any populated area.

Approach each site for a cursory inspection, looking for people or cars that may become too interested in what you're doing. This security check is necessary for the successful implementation of your cache plan. Once you've parked your car near a promising site, sit for a while and take note of pedestrian or automobile traffic. You are going to drive fairly close to your cache site since you'll not only be toting in equipment to dig your hole, but will be carrying your cache in as well.

Once you have found a promising site, look at the road types on all four sides of the section you're considering. Does it appear to be that these roads are well-traveled? Does your potential site have well-trafficked hunting or hiking paths that could possibly expose you and your cache?

Park your car as far in as possible and get out. Don't slam the door (it's good practice so that you learn to be more silent in your activities). Find a tree and sit down for about 10 minutes, and just listen for any problem noises. Take notes of where you're at, get some compass readings, and mark everything down on your map.

## Security

The best security sites are going to be at least a half mile away from your place of work, home, common traveling areas, or any land you may own. Any plot of yours, up to twenty acres, will be searched to a depth of about ten feet if the authorities become suspicious of you. Anything but the lowest security cache (a bucket cache) should be buried outside the places you own or frequent. The upside is that, because of modern materials, nearly any location can be utilized for a hide.

Once you find a site that you like, don't go out and start digging yet. You should survey the area for a while. Is the place you like in bottomland that floods in a simple shower? Is it clay soil or soft moist sandy loam that you'll be digging into?

Another thing you should be careful is knowing who owns the land you're caching on. If you bury your goods on land that's owned by a paper mill, will their equipment unearth or destroy your stash when they start harvesting trees? Is is possible that the land is in an estate that will be sold to a timber company? Will snow totally wipe out all your landmarks come winter?

Think of all the worst-case scenarios that can happen to, and in, the site you've chosen. Only once you're satisfied that conditions are fine or can be handled should you begin the steps needed to bury you cache.

## Tools

What tools will you need to successfully bury a cache? Post-hole diggers and a shovel may get you started, and they'll be good for cleaning out the hole, but they won't be easy to use to dig a hole as deep as you're going to need to bury a 60-inch tube. Remember, you want at least a foot of dirt on top of your cache.

There is a tool called a post auger which is used by farmers and nurseries to dig holes for trees and fence posts. It's made by Seymour Manufacturing Company and the only place I've been able to find it is on Amazon.com. It's called an Iwan Auger and it is the adjustable model.

The nice thing about this auger is that you can easily extend the pipe handle by adding a union and an additional piece of pipe so that you can reach as far as you need to dig your hole. The deeper you go, the harder the digging gets, so plan on being there a while. If you're working in clay soil, try spraying the cutting edges with silicone.

*Iwan Auger*

It will help shed the clay more easily.

There are power augers made today that are hand-held models and can make your job much easier. The only problem is the noise. If you use a power tool in a far-off location, you're going to attract attention to yourself.

You're going to need a tarp of some kind to hold all the loose dirt that you auger out of your hole. The whole point of such careful attention to location and traffic is so that your cache is not discovered. However, if you leave the area looking like a skidder came through there, then you haven't accomplished anything but making the area look suspicious. You must put everything back so that it looks like the earth was never disturbed.

You're going to want some anti-intrusion alarms so that while you're digging and distracted, someone can't inadvertently walk up on you. This can be anything that, if disturbed, will alert you to someone or something in the area. Think in terms of trip wires and some notifying noisemaker.

If you really want to keep people away from you while you are digging, you can buy some imitation skunk scent that you can sprinkle liberally in a large radius around the area you'll be working in. It'll keep people away, but whether you can stay in the area is another story.

Remember, distance from the areas you live in, work in, play in, or frequent is your biggest asset in keeping your cache hidden.

If you place your cache 100 feet out from any of these areas, searchers will have to cover 31,400 square feet in order to thoroughly search for your stuff. This is not a big deal with modern metal detectors. At 200 feet the area to be searched becomes 125,600 square feet—again not a big deal with modern equipment and a team of searchers.

However, move out 1,000 feet and the area to be searched becomes 3.14 million square feet—almost 71 acres! If you scatter decoy metal like nuts and bolts, old cans, nails, and other scrap metal in this area, the searchers would soon tire of false readings and move on.

ஐௌ

Conventional metal detectors are sophisticated equipment. They will find a firearms cache three feet underground all the time. Working harder to avoid discovery is not the answer.

Working smarter is.

> *When the resolution of enslaving America was formed in Great Britain, the British Parliament was advised by an artful man, who was governor of Pennsylvania, to disarm the people; that it was the best and most effectual way to enslave them, but that they should not do so openly, but weaken them, and let them sink gradually...*
>
> George Mason

# CHAPTER 7
## METAL DETECTORS

*The rights of man come not from the generosity of
the state but from the hand of God.*
John F. Kennedy

While metal detectors are not the only equipment that can be used to ferret out a cache, they are one of the most problematic. Metal detectors send out an energy field similar to radio waves. The field reacts to any conductive substance (usually metal), but also mineral deposits and even salty wet ground. The degree of the response is related to the conductivity of the material scanned and the surface area of the material.

The cruder models of the '40s and '60s could be outwitted with strategically placed decoy metal. Today's advanced computerized models, however, allow better trained operators to disregard trash. They automatically compensate for changes in ground conditions as they move over an area. Animal excrement decoys no longer have any affect on the newer models.

They can fine tune their units to find a penny on its edge 18 inches underground. That's why successful caching is a matter of degrees and smart thinking, not the bull-in-the-china-shop approach of scattering decoy metal and urinating all over the place.

Your cache tube, buried horizontally, would make a metal detector sing. However, that same cache tube buried vertically gives a much smaller surface area to read. A gun on its side has almost a square foot of surface area showing. That same gun, muzzle pointing up, has the surface area of a quarter. When you place your cache far out of your sphere of influence, when you bury it with the least amount of surface area showing, when you leave your cache site looking as if the soil has never been disturbed and you pick your site with either isolation or difficulty of detection foremost in your mind, then you've exponentially increased your chances of not being detected.

Again, a matter of degrees is what separates the successful cacher from the one just begging to be discovered.

## How Metal Detectors Work

When you know the principles of how something works, then you can use that understanding and apply it to other situations. By that token, when you understand how a metal detector works, you can devise better ways of avoiding discovery.

Metal detectors use one of three technologies to uncover things:

- Very Low Frequency (VLF)
- Pulse Induction (PI)
- Beat-frequency Oscillation (BFO)

## Very Low Frequency

VLF is also know as induction balance. This is probably the most popular type of metal detector today. A VLF detector has two coils—a transmitter coil and a receiver coil.

The transmitter coil sends out the electronic pulse thousands of times a second, and the reciever coil, acting like an antenna, picks up the frequencies coming from the target objects in the ground.

The electromagnetic field generated pulses back and forth between detector and object. As the detector's field is pulsing downward, the object's field is pulsing upward. The detector can determine how deep the object is based on the strength of the magnetic field it generates.

The farther below the surface the object is, the weaker the field. Beyond a certain depth, the magnetic field of the object is so weak that the receiver coil of the unit can no longer pick it up.

%)(%

How a VLF metal detector differentiates between metals is called phase shifting. Phase shifting is the difference in timing between the frequency of the detector's coils and the frequency of the object scanned. Phase shifting gives VLF metal detectors a capability called discrimination. Because the phase shift is dependent on the conductivity of the material scanned, the trained operator can tell what classification of metals the scanned object belongs to. Some of them even allow the operator to program the detector to disregard certain signatures that belong to things like bottle caps or nails.

## Pulse Induction

PI technology uses powerful short bursts of energy through the detector's coils. It basically creates an echo chamber between the detector and the scanned object. The higher the conductivity of the object scanned, the longer the "echo" of the energy pulse lasts.

PI-based detectors are not very good at discriminating objects scanned because the various echo lengths are not easily separated. However, they are useful in an environment that has highly conductive material—for example, salt water. They can also detect metal much deeper in the ground than other types of detectors.

## Beat-Frequency Oscillation

BFO technology is the very basic of metal detection systems. This system has two coils—one in the head and one inside the control box. Each coil is connected to an oscillator that creates thousands of pulses of energy each second. As these pulses pass through the coils, it creates radio waves.

As this detector passes over a metallic object, the magnetic field that's created between the two coils creates a magnetic field around the object. This magnetic field interferes with the frequency of the radio waves and sends a signal that metal has been found.

These types of detectors are low-cost and can even be built at home.

However, they don't provide the level of accuracy and control that VFI or PI detectors offer.

## Alternate Means of Detection

While there are other means of detection that geophysicists can use (like electromagnetic sensors and gravitational sensors), at a time of societal upheaval that would make accessing your caches necessary, it's unlikely that those means would be used to find a few guns in a pipe "somewhere." Even the ground-penetrating metal detectors that can see 80 feet or deeper are very cost prohibitive and as such, not something in the budget of every local law enforcement agency.

If you have kept yourself off the radar as much as possible, then the chances of law enforcement coming after you diminishes.

## Metal Detector Deterrents

To some extent, minerals and salts in the soil can limit the efficiency and ability of metal detectors. Some areas of the United States have layers of black sand that's composed of nickel-iron

that's hard for metal detectors to penetrate. In fact, most of the western United States has small deposits of black sand, and these would be good sites to check out when you're doing a preliminary site-finding expedition.

In northern Wisconsin and Michigan, iron in the soil will wreak havoc with metal detector readings. However, the clay soil found in Alabama and Mississippi may make detection easier. These soils are more water absorbent and retain that moisture. Water is an excellent conductive material.

It seems like the odds are stacked against being able to successfully cache your weapons, but there are a few more things you can do to swing the pendulum back in your favor. The first one is the rule of squares.

## The Rule of Squares

The rule of squares is a simple mathematical principle that says when you double the distance from a given point, you have four times as much area involved.

As was stated in the last chapter, if you move out 100 feet from your sphere of influence, there's 31,400 square feet of dirt to cover. 200 feet results in 125,600 square feet, almost three acres. At 1,000 feet from your sphere, searching becomes almost hopeless. That's 3.14 million square feet and over 70 acres of dirt to be searched.

Once you've got that big of a space to search, decoy metal can be used. 50 pounds of sixteen-penny nails scattered in the area would be very confusing to say the least.

## Other Places of Difficulty

You should always try to locate your cache in an area that is difficult or impossible to search—where stray dumping, mechanical work, or burying once occurred.

A cemetery is actually one of the best places to bury a cache. If you have access to a rural cemetery, even better. Most are open to the public and can be accessed by car. You can use ponds, streams, marshes, and lakes. Just be sure to glue your end caps on your tubes for these conditions.

ॐ

Do try to avoid reservoirs where the U.S. Corp of Engineers controls the depth of the water for flood control. If you have a season of drought, the reservoir can dry up and anything can be found, most likely by accident.

Some years ago, the flood gates were opened on a reservoir in my area to drain the lake and they found the car and body of a person that had been missing for over 20 years. Tie your cache to the docks or boat ramps in places like this, and you run a high risk of someone else discovering it.

You can place your cache in a place that is impossible to search—for instance, grain silos, in piles of coal, gravel, or under pig pens. Since metal detectors don't work well in close proximity to large amounts of steel, a junk yard or old homestead and farm site would be excellent. Lots of old farms still have rusting tractors and implements sitting on them. Closed garbage dumps are also excellent cache sites.

The best way to avoid metal detectors is to place your cache as far away from you as possible, in a difficult to search place, and keep a low profile. Loose lips are your worst enemy.

ഇരു

# CHAPTER 8
## STAYING BELOW THE RADAR

*Pride goes before destruction,*
*and arrogance before failure.*
Proverbs 16:18

**D**uring WWII, millions were drafted or volunteered for military service. Most of these guys didn't know how to act, what to say, or what to write that would prevent disclosure of sensitive information to the enemy. From this recognition came the motto "Loose lips might sink ships."

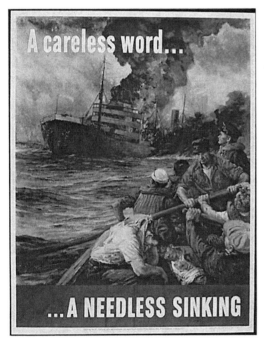

A careless word...
...A NEEDLESS SINKING

It also led to the creation of a multi-point memo of prohibited subjects that the military passed out to all the enlisted men. Some of those points are still good advice for today.

**Don't write down military information on troops—location, strength, material, or equipment.** (Don't write down the locations or contents of your caches. If you must write something down to remember where your hides are, put it in code form and scatter the information among random locations. This ensures that one piece of the information will not give anyone enough knowledge to uncover your caches.)

**Don't mention plans and forecasts, or orders for future operations.** (Don't talk about what you'll do if the government comes to your house. Don't talk about how they'll pry your gun from your cold dead hands. You know

ഈറ

you won't go down without a fight. Don't broadcast intent that can later be used against you.)

**Silence means security...loose talk is direct delivery to the enemy.** (If you want to swagger around, bragging about your "preparations," then by all means do so, but with the understanding that you might as well have just laid your guns out in the front lawn and invited law enforcement or the thugs down the street to come get them.)

Okay, you've been able to acquire a Mini-14 or an AK-47 that you want to cache. But before you put it into your tube, you show it to everybody that comes to the house. Why? If your main goal is to be prepared for whatever breakdown in society may come, why do you want to put your assets on display?

If you don't want people to know that much about you, then don't show them all your toys. What you do in your spare time defines who you are. If you're a hunter, then by all means share your love of the sport with your buddies by talking about recent trophies, or the .270 rifle you had a hard

time sighting in before the last buck you bagged. But don't get into a show-and-tell situation about every long rifle, shotgun, and pistol that you have.

This doesn't just apply to weapons. It applies to wealth and cash as well. When you parade your valuables in public, you come under public scrutiny. You put

yourself in a position of being looked at under a microscope. Even if your buddy has no intention of stealing from you, the bonehead he talks to at work or the bar he frequents may not have such inhibitions. He may try to live vicariously through you by bragging about his friend with all the toys.

## Are You Offering an Invitation?

More than 6 million American homes are burgled each year, about one every 15.4 seconds, according to the FBI. Everyone is a target and no one is immune. If you own a television, a computer, jewelry, or even exotic pets, you have something a thief wants. If you own weapons, you're an even juicier target.

Most burglars are teenagers or young adults under 25 years of age who live in or around your area and have noticed a regular, predictable pattern of your comings and goings. They're looking for an easy target and small stuff that can easily be converted into quick cash. Darkness isn't necessary for burglars, but privacy is. Most will choose an empty house during the daytime  over an occupied one at night. 70% of burglars will use some force to enter a residence, but most prefer an open window or door.

While you may have built your safes, hidey holes, and refuge rooms, you really want to stop the burglar before he gets inside. The first step is to "harden the target," or to make your home more difficult for the thief to enter. Garage and back doors provide more cover, with the garage door being the weakest point of entry.

A burglar will look through your car for keys and valuables, so keep it locked even if it's inside the garage. In addition:

- Use solid core or metal clad doors for all entryways. French doors are particularly weak in a security sense.

ဆာၵ၃

- Use heavy-duty quality deadbolts with a minimum 1" throw-bolt.
- Use heavy-duty doorknob sets that have a dead-latch mechanism to prevent slipping the lock with a credit card.
- Use heavy-duty striker plates with 3-inch screws that will bite into wooden framing members and not just the door trim.
- Use a wide angle, 160° peephole that is no higher than 58 inches from the ground.

Glass paneled doors or glass sliding doors are another weak entry point. Sliding doors do not use locks but latch mechanisms. In older doors, this latch can easily be bypassed by lifting the door up and off the track. There are numerous locking and barring devices for these doors. You should make or purchase one for any sliding glass door in your home.

Windows are more often left unlocked than doors. A burglar may choose your home simply by spotting an open window. Make sure to lock all windows before you leave home. Display decals indicating an alarm system or a dog in high visibility windows and by yard signage. These are deterrents as well.

Never leave a key to the house outside in an obvious or not-so-obvious place. Experienced burglars know all the places to look for these hidden keys. Instead, build a relationship of trust with a neighbor or relative, and leave them a spare key to your house.

Interior lights show that a house is occupied and active at night. A dark home night after night tells people you're either away on vacation or work a second or graveyard shift. A timer is an inexpensive way to keep lights on at night, preferably near front and back windows with the curtains closed. Use these all the time whether you're home or not to establish a pattern and routine. These same timers can be used to turn on television sets and radios to indicate a house is occupied.

Make sure the exterior of your home is well-lit. The new fluorescent spotlights enable you to operate outside security lights for pennies on the dollar compared to the halogen variety. Any thief prefers the shadows where they can enter a home without being spotted. On that same note, trim back shrubbery so that there's no hiding place near the house.

If you're away on vacation, leave a car in your driveway or arrange for a neighbor to leave one there. Have them move it from time to time. Arrange for the yard to be mowed and stop all newspaper and mail deliveries until you return.

## Stay Away From Groups

What was the one factor that led to the tragic circumstances that culminated in the Ruby Ridge massacre? Randy Weaver, along with his wife and children, were isolationists. They lived in a cabin with no electricity or public water source. What made them stand out so much that the FBI staged the raid that led to three deaths?

He joined a group.

If you want to stay below the radar of the government, don't even think about adding your name to a membership roster in any group the government could term a fringe military group, a survivalist group, an unauthorized militia, or a radical terrorist-type organization.

Most groups, like civilian militias, might have hundreds of level-headed members, but it takes just one hot-head to bring the group and all its members down with him. Most people are followers, not leaders, and one belligerent know-it-all can hold sway over the majority.

If there is a cause you believe in then donate funds anonymously. The FBI and ATF routinely infiltrate groups they consider fringe or radical. That guy that seems to be your twin brother separated at birth in viewpoint, and acts like your best friend (who you're spilling all your secrets to) could just be a government agent waiting for the opportunity to arrest you or use you to get to other members.

Remember... loose lips.

> *More burglaries are committed*
> *during the months of*
> *July and August.*
>
> *February has the fewest.*

# CHAPTER 9

# A BIBLICAL RESPONSE TO SELF-DEFENSE, GUNS, AND 2ND AMENDMENT RIGHTS

*The real fire within the builders of America was faith—faith in a provident God whose hand supported and guided them.*
Dwight D. Eisenhower

On a Sunday evening in July of 1993, Charl van Wyk was sitting alone in a pew at St. James Church in Cape Town, South Africa when terrorists entered and began lobbing grenades and shooting parishioners.

Eleven people died and fifty-three people were wounded. However, hundreds more of the almost 1500 people attending the church that night would have perished had not Charl van Wyk returned fire with the .38 special revolver he carried.

But...doesn't the Bible say to turn the other cheek? Aren't we supposed to love our neighbor and give him our cloak, and pay back evil with good? Yes, it does, and we should. But, as with all scripture, care must be given to interpret passages not only within the context of the surrounding scripture, but within the viewpoint of the whole Bible. No passage of scripture renders another null and void. Jesus said he came to fulfill the Law, not do away with it.

The Sermon on the Mount from which Matthew 5:38-39 is taken ("You have heard that our fathers were told, 'Eye for eye and tooth for tooth.' But I tell you not to stand up against someone who does you wrong. On the contrary, if someone hits you on the right cheek, let him hit you on the left cheek too!") deals with righteous personal conduct. Jesus was showing that the authority of government to avenge criminal acts, i.e. punish evildoers, did not give authority to the individual to take revenge. Christ was not teaching something different about self-defense than scripture taught, for didn't he say in the same sermon "Don't think that I have come to abolish the Law or the Prophets. I have come not to abolish but to complete" (Matthew 5:17)? So what does the Bible teach about self-defense?

- Exodus 22:2-3 states "If a thief caught in the act of breaking in is beaten to death, it is not murder; unless it happens after sunrise, in which case it is murder." One can interpret from this scripture that a threat to our lives is to be met with deadly force. The prohibition against killing the thief in the daytime presumes that we can identify and later apprehend the thief if he escapes, and that we are not dealing with a life-threatening situation.

- Proverbs 25:26 states "Like a muddied spring or a polluted well is a righteous person who gives way before the wicked." We falter before the wicked when we do not actively defend ourselves, our loved ones, and innocents against an assailant.

- There is a difference between revenge and resisting attack. Vengeance is the exclusive domain of God and He has given that authority to civilian government, not the individual (Romans 12:19, Romans 13:4). Personal vengeance would entail stalking the criminal down after the threat to our lives was over.

- God in not contradictory and neither are His commandments. The Sixth Commandment tells us "You shall not murder." Yet in the passages following that commandment, God lays out situations where it is perfectly acceptable to protect oneself with lethal force. Clearly this means for the individual, not that we should never kill, but we should not shed innocent blood.

- In the New Testament we learn that Jesus is the same yesterday, today, and forever (Hebrews 13:8). Since Jesus and the Father are one (John 10:30), and God does not change (Malachi 3:6), then nothing in the Old Testament has been replaced or superseded. In fact, Paul states in II Timothy 3:16-17 that all scripture is for doctrine, instruction and correction. Understand that the Gospels, the Acts of the Apostles, and the letters of the New Testament had not been compiled at the time Paul wrote this. Paul clearly was speaking of the Old Testament when making this pronouncement.

෧෬

In fact, this pacifist Christ figure doesn't show up anywhere in the Gospels or the New Testament. The Jesus of the Bible raged against the money lenders in the Temple, he harshly rebuked the religious leaders of his day with sarcasm and venomous remarks. He was confrontational and even rude in a modern, politically incorrect way. He stood toe to toe and eye to eye with the entire Sanhedrin, with

Herod, and with Pilate. These are not the actions of a pacifist or a coward.

In Luke 22:36 we find Jesus instructing his disciples to sell something, even their cloaks, to purchase a sword—a weapon. A Milquetoast caricature of Jesus of Nazareth is a modern-day construct that should be soundly denounced in our churches.

Jesus gave his life freely. He submitted to death on the cross for the sake of salvation and to redeem mankind. He is the essence of love and mercy. However, make no mistake—God is a warrior and He fights for His people.

We are instructed to protect our families and to see to their needs. (I Timothy 5:8). However, it goes even farther than that. The parable of the Good Samaritan shows that we are responsible, if in a position to do so, for the care and protection of our neighbors. Jesus clearly shows the principle of neighborly and just action in this story, condemning those who stood passively by or ignored the victim.

Scripture also shows us the relationship between a nation's righteousness and its willingness and ability to employ self-defense. For example, in

Judges 5:8 we see that the people were oppressed during times of apostasy when "They chose new gods when war was at the gates. Was there a shield or spear to be seen among Israel's forty thousand men?"

In times of national rebellion against the order of God, the rulers of nations will reflect the spiritual degradation of its people by their arrogance, by unlawfully seizing power, and by disarmament and oppression.

Israel under Saul was the same way. Under his rule, the Philistines defeated Israel, disarmed them, and placed them under oppression. (I Samuel 13:19-20, 22-23)

The sword of today is the gun, and we are already seeing entire countries awash in the blood of people killed who had no means to defend themselves. Now these same countries, through the United Nations and treaties passed, want to take away the Second Amendment rights of Americans. Unfortunately, more and more of our legislators feel that the spirit of the Second Amendment applies to national armies only, and not the inherent right of each citizen.

## A Ray of Hope but Remain Vigilant

Since 2006, when the United Nations General Assembly passed the resolution "Toward an Arms Trade Treaty," there has been a growing suspicion that such a treaty might be used as a "back door" for control in the United States. For several years now the UN has been hosting sessions to obtain the views of member states concerning "...the feasibility, scope, and draft parameters for a comprehensive, legally binding instrument establishing common international standards for the import, export, and transfer of conventional arms." That resolution was approved 153-1 with only the U.S. dissenting. In 2008, the UN General Assembly passed a similar resolution with the U.S. again voting "No."

Since President Obama took office, the U.S. has shown renewed interest in the notion of an international arms treaty. What sets such a treaty apart is that, unlike nuclear weapons agreements, this treaty is aimed specifically at hand guns and other small arms. The proposal being considered carries with it sweeping restrictions on small arms trade and hefty penalties for violations by American gun owners.

Secretary of State Hillary Clinton recently issued a statement saying: "The United States is committed to actively pursuing a strong and robust treaty that contains the highest possible, legally binding standards for the international transfer of conventional weapons." And on October 28, 2010, the General Assembly voted 153-1 to move forward in preparation for a United Nations conference on the arms trade treaty in 2012 that could yield a formal document. This time, Zimbabwe was the lone dissenter with 19 nations abstaining.

Thankfully opposition has finally risen to President Obama's and Secretary of State Hillary Clinton's vocal support for the United Nations proposal to control guns within the borders of the United States and other nations around the world. There are currently 55 senators, including 10 Democrats, who have signed letters of intention to oppose any such treaty should the President present it to them.

Kansas Republican Senator Jerry Moran, an author of one such letter, warns: "Our country's sovereignty and the Second Amendment rights of American citizens must not be infringed upon by the United Nations. Today, the Senate sends a powerful message to the Obama Administration: an Arms Trade Treaty that does not protect ownership of civilian firearms will fail in the Senate. Our firearm freedoms are not negotiable."

While supporters of the treaty contend the goal of the treaty is to author internationally recognized rules to govern the trade of guns and ammunition, opponents rightfully view it as the first step toward home-grown gun control. Groups like the National Rifle Association believe it would allow for international authorities to control American gun ownership. The NRA writes of the treaty:

> As we have for the past 15 years, the NRA will fight to stop a United Nations Arms Trade Treaty that infringes on the constitutional rights of the American gun owner. [The Moran letter] sends a clear message to the international bureaucrats who want to eliminate our fundamental, individual right to keep and bear arms. Clearly, a U.N. Arms Trade Treaty that includes civilian arms within its scope is not supported by the American people or their elected U.S. Senators. Senator Moran is a true champion of our freedom. We are grateful for his leadership and his tenacious efforts on this issue, as well as the 44 other senators who agree with the NRA's refusal to compromise on our constitutional freedoms.

Many groups, like FactCheck.org, fail to see the implications of such a treaty. It categorically denies assertions a UN treaty would infringe on Second Amendment rights, saying, "the idea that a treaty necessarily would make U.S. citizens subject to those gun laws created by foreign governments is wrong. Treaties don't subject one nation's citizens to the laws of other nations. They do commit governments to whatever actions a treaty specifies, such as ceasing to test nuclear weapons."

John Bolton, former ambassador to the UN, disagrees.

> The administration is trying to act as though this is really just a treaty about international arms trade between nation states, but there's no doubt—as was the case back over a decade ago— that the real agenda here is domestic firearms control. After the treaty is approved and it comes into force, you will find out that it … requires the Congress to adopt some measure that restricts ownership of firearms. The administration knows it cannot obtain this kind of legislation purely in a domestic context.…They will use an international agreement as an excuse to get domestically what they couldn't otherwise.

෪෬

He knows firsthand how seemingly innocuous international treaties become stepping stones to altering internal government affairs. President Obama wouldn't be the first U.S. leader to use a signed treaty as justification for perusing further actions. FactCheck and other such groups embrace the delusion that the current administration is softer on gun control than most first thought it would be. Incidents like the Gunwalker Scandal prove that President Obama is more than willing to look for back-door methods to achieve his ideological goals. Hopefully those 55 Senators will remain united and close the door on the United Nations' attempt to tamper with our Constitution.

## "Fast and Furious"—a Case in Point

A prime example of how the current administration attempts an end run on gun control is what has been tagged the "Gunwalker Scandal." The Bureau of Alcohol, Tobacco and Firearms carried out a supposed sting operation labeled "Fast and Furious" that not only went horribly awry, but illustrates how far a president and government officials will go to ensure acceptance of their agenda. An outline of "Fast and Furious" is as follows:

- U.S. gun dealers were instructed by the ATF to allow questionable and illegal sales of firearms to suspected gunrunners.

- ATF agents allowed, and even assisted, those guns to cross the U.S. border into Mexico to "boost the number" of American civilian market firearms seized in Mexico. This was done to provide justification for additional firearm restrictions on American citizens and funnel more authority and money to the ATF.

- Against the objection of some conscientious ATF agents, Mexican authorities were deliberately kept in the dark about the operation.

- Weapons the ATF enabled to walk into Mexico were subsequently used in the murders of Border Patrol Agent Brian Terry and ICE agent Jaime Zapata, as well as hundreds of Mexican citizens.

- Since the murder of Brian Terry in December 2010, the Obama administration has been engaged in an aggressive cover-up of the facts behind what is now known as the "Gunwalker Scandal."

℘℞

It is refreshing to know there are still a few men of honor, such as Kenneth Melson, acting director of the Bureau of Alcohol, Tobacco, Firearms, and Explosives, proved. When complications arose with the scheme, Melton refused to be a sacrificial lamb in order to draw attention away from the Department of Justice and President Obama. Rather than step down, he exposed the operation for what it was—an attempt to influence Americans' views of gun control by enabling Mexican drug cartels to purchase legally sold weapons in the United States.

Melton revealed just how far the administration was willing to go to achieve its gun control agenda. What unfolded was a program funded by over $100 million dollars of "stimulus" money and led by the ATF to solicit buyers to purchase hundreds of weapons from legally licensed gun shops in border states. The idea was the guns could somehow be traced back to Mexican drug cartels across the border in Mexico. There has yet to be an explanation of how U.S. ATF agents could trace weapons in another sovereign country without its knowledge. The Justice Department stands by its claim "Fast and Furious" was simply a sting operation that failed, but such cannot possibly be the case. The ATF has no authority to track guns inside Mexico without that country's approval. Therefore, the operation must have originated far above the ATF's authority level.

Attorney General Eric Holder testified to a congressional committee in March 2011 that he knew about "Fast and Furious" for less than a month before the hearings. Considering Holder suggested this kind of operation to a joint Mexico-U.S. law enforcement conference in Mexico two years earlier, it is obvious the truth is not being told.

Acting Director Melson related a very different story when he spoke before congressional investigators. In his testimony, he revealed the existence of internal memos from Obama political appointees in the Justice Department that had been withheld from Congress. He also has testified that the Justice Department officially denied the existence of the sting operation while at the same time procuring wire tap authorization to carry out "Fast and Furious."

ॐ

Melson told investigators that during Operation Fast and Furious, guns were bought by and sold to individuals connected with the Mexican cartels who were also paid informants for the FBI and the Drug Enforcement Administration. American taxpayers are funding all sides of this war. Not only has the U.S. Congress begun investigations, but so has their counterpart in Mexico as well. Some within the Mexican government are even calling the Obama operation an act of war. At least 200 Mexican law enforcement and military personnel have been killed in the last year by guns traced directly to "Fast and Furious."

The example of the UN treaty and operation "Fast and Furious" should serve as a cautionary illustration of how vigilant we as citizens must be concerning our Second Amendment rights.

# CHAPTER
## CONCLUSION

*Man will ultimately be governed by*
*God or by tyrants.*
Benjamin Franklin

**W**hen we hear about things like the UN Treaty for Arms Control or government operations funneling legally bought American weapons into Mexico, the first questions has to be "Why?" What is the motivation for such actions?

George W. Bush entered into a treaty with the Canadian and Mexican governments on March 23, 2005. Bush skirted congressional approval by signing the treaty into effect by executive order. The meeting was held at Baylor University in Waco, Texas. This meeting saw President Bush, Vicente Fox of Mexico, and Canadian Prime Minister Paul Martin sign the SPP (Security and Prosperity Partnership) agreement that allows Canadian or Mexican troops to enter the United States to quell any uprising or civil unrest. George W. Bush, on March 23, 2005, signed away all vestiges of national sovereignty and the constitutional rights of the people of the United States of America.

Barak Obama has simply sought to ratchet up tensions and therefore move Americans toward acceptance of gun control laws they have formerly been resistant to. With violence spilling across our borders as the war between the Mexican government and drug cartels escalates, it is inevitable the results will be blamed on lack of gun control in the United States. Secretary of State Hillary Clinton, Director of Homeland Security Janet Napolitano, and President Obama have all publicly called attention to border violence and blamed it on soft gun control in U.S. gun shops and gun shows along the border.

ജയ

There can be no doubt an orchestrated attempt is being made to fan the flames of gun violence and thus create a public outcry for stricter gun control laws. The supposed reason will be to protect Mexican and American citizens, but the real reason is to promote an agenda.

The Justice Department is still blaming gun shops in southwestern states for the violence along their borders. A crisis was created, and now the ATF has announced a new measure requiring all gun shops in border states to report purchases of two or more of some types of rifles by the same person in a five-day span. The Justice Department describes this as an effort to stop the illicit flow of weapons into Mexico, but it is the ATF that helped increase the flow to begin with.

The agenda for such an operation goes far beyond gun control. Guns traced back to "Fast and Furious" ended up with the Zeta drug cartel which has active plans to disrupt Mexico's 2012 elections.  All of this is most disturbing because of the way this is being framed to allow for the inclusion of the State Department and CIA in what was supposed to be a method to halt gun violence within our borders. The CIA, in particular, has a history of inserting itself into the affairs of foreign governments in order to "protect American interests." "Fast and Furious" purposefully allowed gun trafficking to violent drug cartels that know nothing of national borders and would be glad to pull down governments on both side of the border if they could.

It's no longer a matter of "if" the American people will be disarmed, it's a matter of "when." The only hope we have is to return this country to the republic it was, consisting of constitutional rights and law.

Unfortunately the people of America have grown lazy. We no longer have that frontiersman "can-do" attitude. We look to government to provide instead of God and our own two hands. We wallow in a cesspool of victimhood and entitlement.

We're too apathetic to stay abreast of what our government is doing.

Those of us who still adhere to the vision the Founding Fathers had of this

෫ඏ

nation are the last vanguard standing between freedom and oppression. We need to work tirelessly through government channels to elect men and women of like values, and through the courts to petition on behalf of the American people for adherence to constitutional principles. However, once those options are no longer open to us, then we may have to ask ourselves, as did Patrick Henry, "Is life so dear or peace so sweet as to be purchased at the price of chains and slavery? Forbid it, Almighty God!"

How well we prepare now, as individual citizens across the land, will determine how well we stand against future tyrannies, whether civilian or government in nature, whether foreign or domestic in design.

*I love the man that can smile in trouble, that can gather strength from distress, and grow brave by reflection. 'Tis the business of little minds to shrink; but he whose heart is firm, and whose conscience approves his conduct, will pursue his principles unto death.*

*These are the times that try men's souls. The summer soldier and the sunshine patriot will, in this crisis, shrink form the service of his country; but he that stands it now, deserves the love and thanks of man and woman.*

*Thomas Paine, The American Crisis, No. 1*
*December 19, 1776*

# RESOURCES FOR CACHE MATERIALS

VCI paper can be purchased at several online sites. Go to www.uline.com or www.packingsupplies.com, two different sites that sell this material. There are also surplus dealers on eBay that auction off VCI paper from time to time at a much cheaper price. Go to www.ebay.com and type in "VCI paper" in the search box to see current auctions.

Plastic sleeving large enough to fit over long rifles can be purchased at several places online as well. Two places to check out are www.uline.com and www.polybagsupplies.com. They both offer reasonable prices.

Silica can be bought in packets or in bulk. Again, www.uline.com seems to be the packaging supercenter when it comes to these types of supplies. Of course, you can always do your own Internet search to see if you can obtain it cheaper somewhere else.

Military medical kits can be found at two different places: www.afmo.com and www.theepicenter.com. They have more than your standard first aid supplies. There are also auctions from time to time on eBay as well, so check there regularly.

Your local tax assessor's office will have the tax maps for your area that will tell you the ownership of property you're interested in. In addition, they may have the topographical maps for your area. If your county doesn't carry them, you can contact the U.S. Department of the Interior to purchase them.

# IMPORTANT RESOURCES
# PRODUCTS FOR SELF-RELIANT LIVING

## Paratrooper Water Filter

This filter gives you the ability to enjoy clean water anywhere, at any time. Super lightweight and ultra-compact, this water filter goes everywhere you want to go. It removes 100% of harmful water-borne bacteria, toxic metals, and other unwanted contaminants, including *e.coli*. The Paratrooper water filter is light enough to carry in your backpack, glove box, or purse. Leaves you with only the freshest tasting, crystal clear water. Find out more about the Paratrooper water filter at: www.bestlittlefilter.com

## Crisis Cooker

Ever wanted to find a way to cook hot, healthy meals for your family, even when the power goes out? The Crisis Cooker is a highly efficient charcoal, wood, or propane cooker that allows you to boil, grill, fry, or bake at any time, in any given situation. The Crisis Cooker is portable, easy to use, and comes fully assembled. It's an essential part of your family's emergency preparedness plan. To learn more about this revolutionary cooker, visit: www.crisiscooker.com

## Evac Pack

If a natural disaster or an emergency forced you to leave home quickly, would you and your family be prepared to go at a moment's notice? Not every crisis gives you a warning…(remember the Japan earthquake and tsunami just months ago?) In those situations, you need to be able to grab some essential supplies and evacuate within minutes, if not seconds. The Evac Pack is an easy-to-carry bag filled with essential foods and the basic supplies you'll need to survive in any kind of short-term survival situation. While you can't predict an emergency, you CAN prepare for one. To see this amazing grab n' go bag, visit: www.myevacpack.com

## Food Shortage Buckets (emergency meals)

Nobody likes to think about going hungry. Skipping a single meal is an unpleasant thought in today's culture. But what if your family had to go for days, or even weeks, without food? Unless you are prepared for a crisis or emergency situation, you and your family could be at risk. It's never been more important to have an emergency food supply on hand, ready to feed your family in any situation. These food storage buckets are packed with nutritionally dense, healthy, and delicious emergency meals your family is guaranteed to love. Even better, these meals have an extended shelf life and will not spoil. They'll be ready when you need them most. Don't wait until it's too late. Order your meals today at: www.foodshortagesolutions.com

## Heirloom Solutions (heirloom seed site)

Growing healthy, nutritious food in your own backyard has never been easier. Home gardening has become a popular activity and with good reason. Heirloom Solutions gives you the tools you need to grow the very best organic, heirloom varieties of plants that will nourish and feed your family. They stock a large variety of the best quality heirloom seeds to meet all your needs. From vegetables to herbs, to lettuces and beans…they have everything you need to garden organically. To see their extensive catalog and seed selection, visit: www.heirloomsolutions.com

## Herb Bank (herb seed kit)

For thousands of years, civilizations have flourished using herbal remedies to treat common ailments and serious diseases. These remedies have stood the test of time, being handed down for generations. Learning how to grow and make your own herbal remedies is a wise choice for your health care needs, but it's also a good way to save money! Most herbal remedies are inexpensive and easy to make. The Survival Herb Bank includes 20 powerful herbs that will give you the capacity to treat colds, cough, flu, PMS, allergies and more—all from the comfort of your home. To learn more, visit: www.survivalherbbank.com

## Summer Survival Mat

The Summer Survival Mat supports your body's own natural cooling mechanism. The secret is in the patent-pending gel inside the mat. The non-toxic, water-based gel actually absorbs your body heat. Once the Summer Survival Mat has reached its heat absorption capacity, simply set it aside in a cool area of your home and the gel will automatically "reset" for the next use. It works efficiently in environments up to 86 degrees, and requires no power or electricity to work. Stay cool no matter what. Visit http://www.cooldownfast.com

## Drag and Draw Gun Vault

Worried about intruders or home invasion? Most gun owners want to find a way to keep their handgun locked and loaded, ready for instant use—without fear of an accident. The truth is, an assailant will not give you time to find and load your gun. To be prepared for anything, you simply must keep you firearms ready at all times. The Drag and Draw Gun Vault is an exceptional way to keep your handgun out of sight, yet readily accessible. It is equipped with biometric technology that keeps anyone but you from opening it. To learn more, visit: www.myquicksafe.com

## Protogrow

Protogrow is an all-new, all-natural fertilizer that boosts your garden production to levels you've never experienced before. In fact, Protogrow has the potential to more than double your harvest and crop yields! This amazing fertilizer is the perfect addition to your organic gardening routines and practices. It's so powerful it almost forces your plants to grow in any kind of condition. Try it today at www.growlikecrazy.com

## Survival Seed Bank (heirloom seed kit)

How would you like to grow enough food to feed your family, friends, and even neighbors for years and years to come? The Survival Seed Bank is a special collection of hard to find, open-pollinated super seeds that will produce for you year after year. When the grocery shelves are empty, your family will be enjoying delicious and hearty vegetables straight from your own "crisis garden." Each seed has been carefully selected for longevity, and these seeds have a very long shelf life. Buy this seed bank once, and never worry about your food security again. Check it out at: www. survivalseedbank.com

## Peruvian Sleep Generator

Maybe you have trouble falling asleep. Or, perhaps a night of deep, restful sleep seems impossible for you. If you have trouble falling asleep, this may be the most important product you'll ever purchase. This breakthrough CD contains a pattern of "synergistic" recorded sounds called *binaural beats* that are proven to help you sleep. The unique audio CD recording produces perfectly safe and non-addictive sleep that works almost instantly. To learn more about this amazing product, visit: www. highspeedsleep.com

## Solar Generators

Hurricanes. Snow storms. Ice storms. Brownouts or blackouts. The next time a major weather event happens, will you be left in the dark? What about an emergency or crisis that crashes the electric grid? A solar powered generator will keep your lights on in any of these situations...and for free. (No power company owns the sun!) These plug-and-play solar generators are highly efficient and made in the USA. These generators are portable and give you power where and when you need it most. No disaster or emergency preparedness plan is complete without one. Request your free informational packet and learn more at: www.mysolarbackup.com

## Solar Oven

Harness the power of the sun to cook delicious meals anywhere, anytime. No wood? No gas? No electricity? NO PROBLEM. The Solar Oven needs nothing more than daylight to work. With a solar oven you can cook just about anything so long as the sun is shining. And, with the built-in thermometer, you can make sure your food is cooked thoroughly so it is 100% safe to eat. The Solar Oven is portable, durable, and extremely affordable in the long run (there's never any cost in fuel). It's perfect for survival, or for camping and outdoor activities. Buy it once and use it forever. To learn more, visit: www.bestsolaroven.com

## Survival Sprout Bank (seeds for sprouts)

In a crisis situation, your health is everything. These days, more and more people are stockpiling food and preparing for hard times. Yet, most folks have no real source of phytonutrients, those living nutrients like vitamins, minerals, and enzymes, in their pantry. Sprouts will give you and your family a continual, renewable source of these essential enzymes. This secret "superfood" could make or break your chances of surviving—and thriving—through a crisis. The Survival Sprout Bank includes everything you need to grow (and store) 10 carefully selected sprout varieties for maximum nutritional value. Easy to use, easy to grow. Learn more at: www. survivalsproutbank.com

## Stove In A Can

Stove In A Can is a self-contained, revolutionary cooking platform that can be used for emergency preparedness, outdoor recreation, and more. Virtually anything that can be cooked on a regular stove can be cooked on a Stove In A Can. It's lightweight and easy to transport. Includes four fuel cells that are waterproof and windproof. Just light the fuel cell, and you're cooking within minutes. To see this amazing, compact stove, visit: http://www.solutionsfromscience.com/?p=1819

## LED light bulbs

The Energy Saver Bundle includes five LED light bulbs that cast the same amount of light as 60-watt incandescent bulbs, but use only one-tenth of the energy. Each LED bulb gives off pure, white light and can last up to 40 years! These durable, energy-efficient bulbs fit standard size light bulb sockets. Unlike compact fluorescent bulbs, they contain no mercury and are non-toxic in the event of breakage. Order your bundle today at: http://www.solutionsfromscience.com/?p=1684

## Potassium Iodide tablets

After the Fukishima meltdown in Japan, many Americans vowed to never let themselves be unprepared for a radiation fallout situation. Potassium Iodide tablets should be a staple in your family survival kit. Each bottle contains fourteen 130-mg tablets of potassium iodide, enough for one adult for two weeks. For temporary, emergency use only. When used as instructed by a health care professional, potassium iodide safely provides iodine to the receptor sites of the thyroid gland, blocking the uptake of potentially harmful radioactive iodine in a radiation exposure emergency. Not for use by individuals with a thyroid condition or iodine sensitivity. Order your tablets today at: http://www.solutionsfromscience.com/?p=2108

## 72-hour Emergency Meal Kit

Want a way to feed your family in a crisis situation? The 72-hour Emergency Meal kit will keep 1 person fed for 3 days. All pouches are "cook in the pouch" entrees. You'll receive Pasta Alfredo, Cheesy Lasagna, Savory Stroganoff, Teriyaki and Rice, Creamy Pasta and Vegetable Rotini, and Chili Macaroni. These kits are in high demand so order yours today at: http://www.solutionsfromscience.com/?p=1562

## Nitro Seed Starter

This amazing product allows you to jump start your crops. Simply soak your seeds in this solution for a few seconds before planting. The seeds will just grow like crazy! A great addition to your organic gardening supplies. Find out more at: http://www.solutionsfromscience.com/?p=814

## Chia—the Survival Superfood

The amazing Aztec "superfood," used for hundreds of years by native tribes for strength and endurance. Saved from extinction by a remote Native American tribe, hand-grown and cultivated, this nutritional powerhouse is now available to you for your survival stores. Chia is the richest, non-marine source of omega-3 fats found anywhere on the planet and is packed with protein, vitamins, and minerals. It also contains ALL the essential amino acids that make up complete proteins. Order your supply of chia seed at: http://www.survivalsuperfoods.com.

ഇൻൻ

## Gift Cards

Let those you love select the gifts they want most! Solutions from Science offers many products that complement your "off the grid" and self-sufficient lifestyle. From garden items to survival supplies, to books, DVDS and more, the recipient of your gift card will find something they're sure to love. Gift cards come in $10, $25, $50, and $100 amounts. Purchase a gift card today at: http://www.solutionsfromscience.com/?cat=56

# IMPORTANT RESOURCES
## BOOKS AND DVDS

### Canning DVDs

Food prices are skyrocketing and the entire food system is fragile enough it could completely crumble with any emergency or crisis. Many people are busy preparing to feed their families in lean times or in the event of empty store shelves. This DVD set contains absolutely everything you need to know to put up food for you family. Canning, dehydrating, and other methods of storing food for your family are covered in the *Food Storage Secrets* set of 3 DVDs. Learn everything you need to know, from safety measures to the best things you should preserve for your family, right now. It's the ultimate crash course in food preservation! Visit www.foodshortageusa.com to learn more.

### 77 Items Gone from Grocery Store Shelves

This special report could prove to be the one thing that keeps your family fed in the event of a major crisis or emergency. Learn what essential items you should be stockpiling (and those you shouldn't) in your home in case the shelves at the grocery store run dry. Even veteran "survivalists" have learned much from this special report.  Before the next hurricane, earthquake or other natural disaster hits, learn more at: www.preparedforcrisis.com

### Emergency Herbs

Discover how to make your own emergency herbal remedies—perfect for use in any survival situation or when medical help may be unavailable or unaffordable. This book will show you exactly which herbs could be lifesavers for you and your family, and is an easy-to-read, quick crash course in emergency herbal medicine. From coughs and sore throats, to fevers and flu, this book contains the information you may desperately need one day. To learn more about this important book, visit: www.emergencyherbs.com

## Founders Plan

Are you worried about Obamacare? Concerned about the dismal state of affairs in America? Consider yourself a patriot? Or perhaps you just want to learn how to successfully debate and dialogue with the socialists and agenda-driven political spin masters amongst us. Introducing the 6-CD set: *The Crash Course on the U.S. Constitution: How to Argue with a Liberal about Constitutional Issues—and Win Every Time!* Quickly learn the real truth behind the U.S. Constitution, and be able to beat liberals at their own game. To read more about these informative CDs visit: www.thefoundersplan.com

## Gold Buyers Manual

The USA is in the midst of a major economic meltdown. As the country's financial situation continues to swirl down the proverbial drain, many concerned citizens are looking for a legitimate way to guarantee financial safety for their family. Have you ever wanted to buy gold as an investment, but were too scared to get started? Are you worried about getting taken advantage of? Look no further. This book is for you: *How to Buy Gold... Without Getting Ripped Off*. It is a vital resource that will help see that your family is on solid financial ground. Learn more at: www.nomoregoldscams.com

## Make Herbal Medicines

Learn how to make powerful herbal medicines in the comfort of your own kitchen! This complete how-to course includes 3 DVDs of quality hands-on instruction and a 150-page reference manual. When you finish the course, you'll know more about the preparation of herbs and herbal medicines than 99.9% of the doctors in this country. Given the current status of the health care system, it could turn out to be some of the most precious information you'll ever learn. Visit www.makeherbalmedicines.com to learn more.

## Martial Law

*Understanding and Surviving Martial Law* is much more than a history lesson. This book is packed with valuable, practical information that will empower you to survive and even thrive during a time of martial law. This book will give you the tools you'll desperately need to protect yourself, your family, and your property in the event of a police state. Learn the "Five Martial Law Rules to Live By" that every person should memorize. Visit www.martiallawsurvival.com to learn more about this important book.

## Make Money with Your Truck

Need a little extra cash? How about a lot of extra cash? Perhaps you're out of work and need to find a source of income. You can now use inside information to make a good living with a piece of equipment you already own—your truck. This book will teach you how to leverage what you've already got to help others...and get some quick cash that will leave others wondering where all the money came from. Go to www.moneywithyourtruck.com for more information about this exciting income possibility!

## The Only Way Back

Imagine tanks rolling down your neighborhood streets, black uniformed troops marching behind them, soldiers knocking on doors and searching homes without warrants or even reasonable suspicion. Sound far-fetched? It may not be, should America continue down this slope of moral decline. For those of us who are ready to see America return to her Christian roots, the *Christian Liberty or Martial Law* kit is a must-have. This book and CD set will help you see the only way back to America as our Founders wanted it. To order this revolutionary and informative set, visit: www.theonlywayback.com

## Pale Horse

Chemical and biological attacks on American soil? It could happen, and sooner than you may think. The bottom line: Our nation is wide open to a chemical weapon or biological sneak attack, the likes of which could

ଽଚ୰

make Pearl Harbor and 9/11 pale in comparison. Because of this, every home should have this book on their shelves: *Pale Horse: How to Survive a Chemical or Biological Attack*. In this book you'll learn exactly what signs to look for, and how to act in the event of a biological or chemical attack. You'll learn what the real threats are and how to protect those you love. This is not your father's survival handbook! Order today at www.biowarsurvival.com

## Red Horse

The recent earthquake, tsunami, and nuclear meltdown events in Japan have prompted many Americans to educate themselves about the possibility of radiation fallout on American soil. If you've ever wanted to know how to survive a dirty bomb blast, an atomic explosion, or even a nuclear reactor meltdown, then you need to read *Red Horse: How to Survive a Nuclear Blast or Dirty Bomb* today. This book will cover everything you need to know to survive a dirty bomb or radiation blast. Learn how to prepare your home right now and what to do before, during, and after a radiation event. Visit www.dirtybombsurvival.com for more information.

## Silver Buyers Manual

It's no secret. The economy has gone to hell in a handbasket, and it doesn't look like it's going to get better any time soon. Massive federal debts, empty state budgets, the housing market meltdown, and now the downgraded credit rating of the USA. It's no wonder that many people believe that it's going to get worse before it gets better. Many Americans are looking to buy gold, but have found that they can't scrape together the thousands of dollars to get started. This manual was written expressly for those folks. *The Silver Buyers Manual* will teach you how to acquire wealth—in silver, the right way. No gimmicks, no tricks. Just real, easy-to-understand knowledge. Learn more today: www.silvermanual.com

## Survival Stockpiling

Take a look at your kitchen cabinets right now. How long could you get by without going to the store? A week? A month? If a crisis happened, would you find yourself in a soup line the next day? It's something every person should stop and think about. *Survival Stockpiling: How to Make Sure There Is Food On The Table When All Hell Breaks Loose* may be one of the most important books on food stockpiling you'll ever read. It will help you calculate exactly how much food you need to have on hand, and what foods you should stock and those to avoid. This book even includes exact shopping lists to take with you to the market for reference. Learn more at: www.survivalstockpiling.com

## Tax Lien Insider

One of the few investments not affected by the interest rates set by the Federal Reserve bankers, one of the few investments not affected by the roller coaster ride of the stock market, and one of the few investments that cannot be manipulated by Washington insiders and special interests—and with as little as $100, you can start making these investments today. What are we talking about? Tax liens. No, we're not talking about stealing someone's home and tossing them out in the street. Many property owners get into a bind and can't pay their taxes. Local governments then put the properties up for sale for back taxes. Only the property owner has anywhere from 2 to 3 years to get his back taxes paid up. You're basically lending folks money to pay their taxes, and when they do settle up with the county courthouse, you get your money back, with interest. Want to learn more? Go to http://www.taxlieninsider.com.

## Agenda DVD

The documentary *Agenda* is the perfect "antidote" for socialism. It not only explains the roots of socialism in America, but also what we can do to take our country back and restore freedom and liberty, perhaps even in our lifetimes. Buy a copy for your own family today. Visit: http://www.solutionsfromscience.com/?p=809

## Homestead Blessings: The Art of Herbs DVD

For thousands of years, herbs have been used to make salves, tinctures, healing medicines, and even for enhancing the flavor of food. *The Art of Herbs*, an in-depth DVD that teaches you just about everything you ever wanted to know about identifying, growing, storing, and using herbs for both culinary and health-enriching purposes. The West Ladies of Homestead Blessings farm reveal their herb gardening secrets and show you how to make your own vinegars, teas, butters, and more. Buy your copy today at: http://www.solutionsfromscience.com/?p=807

## Homestead Blessings: The Art of Gardening DVD

Most Americans are out-of-touch with where their food comes from. When we buy our food at the grocery store, most of us eat it without ever really thinking about how it arrived on our kitchen table. Is it any surprise so few people still know the lost secrets of organic gardening? The West Ladies of Homestead Blessings farm have been growing their own food, flowers, and plants for many years, and have a wealth of "down home" knowledge about the art of gardening. In this DVD, they share their secrets about composting, pest control, potato patches, flowers, container gardening, vegetables, climate conditions, and much more! *The Art of Gardening* DVD is an excellent addition to your home library. Order today at: http://www. solutionsfromscience.com/?p=805

## The Christian and Civil Government

*The Christian and Civil Government*, by Pastor John Weaver, is a theological treatise on Romans 13. This book explains the Christian's responsibility and relationship to civil government. The book exposes corrupt, unbiblical and ungodly civil government…and teaches you to discern for yourself. Pastor Weaver has been in the Christian ministry for over 40 years and is considered an expert on this subject. Order your copy today at: http://www.solutionsfromscience.com/?p=1294

## Christianity and the Constitution

*Christianity and the Constitution* explores the Christian influence upon America's greatest document, the Constitution. This book will bring you back to the roots that made America great in the first place. It is legally accurate and easy to understand (which is no small feat). Every student of American history should read this book. Order yours today at: http://www. solutionsfromscience.com/?p=1284

ᔓᗏᔕᗕ

## Get Out of Debt

In debt? Tired of bill collectors calling at all hours? If this is you, or someone you love, you owe it to yourself to check out the *The Debtor's Secret Weapon*. This program is guaranteed to slash your debt and eliminate bill collectors quickly. It is very easy to use, and best of all, it will only take only a few minutes to do...get out of debt in less than 90 minutes! These materials will teach you how to get out of debt without filing bankruptcy or taking out more loans. Don't worry—this is no "shady" credit repair program. It's completely legitimate, and it really works! Find out more at: www.outin90.com

## Emergency Herbs

After buying and reading 72 books about herbs and herbal remedies, all the best information was distilled down into this must-have guide about making herbal medicines. This amazing "little" book reveals 15 herbs you should always have on hand, how to cheaply make your own herbal remedies at home, and more. No home library should be without this valuable resource. Learn more at: http://www.solutionsfromscience.com/?p=771

## For You They Signed

In 1776, 56 men signed their names on a document that changed the world forever. Standing on principles of faith and liberty, these men forged a powerful call for freedom and human dignity that is still heard today in America. The book, *For You They Signed,* is a volume of life-changing devotional character studies. Perfect for family or group studies. Order your copy today at: http://www.solutionsfromscience.com/?p=1301

## George Washington Carver DVD

The inspiring documentary film, *George Washington Carver: An Uncommon Way* is an excellent addition to your family DVD library. Carver, born a slave in 1864, was a natural inventor. During his life, Carver developed more than 300 different products from the peanut; 175 from the sweet potato; and 60 from the pecan. He was passionate about helping the poor and was a champion of social justice. This film will give your family much to discuss and ponder. Order at: http://www.solutionsfromscience.com/?p=803

## Hero Set

This four book set includes: *Life of Washington, Life of Luther, Life of John Knox,* and *Life of Andrew Jackson.* Makes an excellent addition to your family library. A great way to combine history with character training. Order your set today at: http://www.solutionsfromscience.com/?p=1653

## Legacy of Liberty and Property

*The Legacy of Liberty and Property In The Story Of American Colonization and The Founding Of A Nation*—a look at the amazing story of freedom that stemmed from the Reformation in the 1500s, that prevailed throughout America's colonial era, and that culminated in the formation of a free nation. It covers the historic wall of separation between family and state and shows that a nation which was conceived in independence was never intended to make dependents of its citizens.

## Ready For Anything (No B.S. Survival Manual)

Most of the time, catastrophes happen without any warning. Will you be prepared for any survival situation? I'm not talking about having a flashlight and extra batteries handy. I'm talking about being prepared enough to survive completely on your own for days on end. The *Ready For Anything (No B.S. Survival Manual)* is not your grandfather's survival book. It is a completely up-to-date resource detailing everything you need to know for a potential survival situation. Take the steps outlined in this book and you will have far better odds of surviving and thriving during a time of crisis. Don't panic, be prepared. Buy your manual today at: www.readyforanythingmanual.com

## Survival Gardening with Heirlooms

This book is designed to help anyone—beginner or expert—cultivate a highly productive crisis garden. Written by a survivalist and a master gardener, it describes in detail, each step of the way, taking you by the hand from planting your seeds, to cultivating, to gathering and storing your seeds for the next growing season. An excellent companion to the Survival Seed Bank! Order today at: http://www.solutionsfromscience.com/?p=794

## Dialogues of Fenelon (Lamp Lighters books)

This wonderful devotional will bless you with simple reminders of God's eternal truths. This high quality book is pocket size and leatherbound, and will be a prized book in your family library. Order today at: http://www. solutionsfromscience.com/?p=2102

## The Homesteading Handbook

Wherever you live—farm, suburb, or even city—*The Homesteading Handbook* will show you how to embrace a more self-sufficient lifestyle. Learn to plant and harvest your own organic garden. Plus, you'll learn how to enjoy fruits and vegetables year round by canning, drying, and freezing. From beekeeping to basket weaving to baking, this handy guide has everything you need to operate your own little homestead. Find out more at: http://www.solutionsfromscience.com/?p=2082

## Keeping Chickens

You don't need a large space to keep chickens, and most families find that they only need a couple of hens to keep them stocked with fresh eggs year-round. This handbook will teach you the basics such as: housing costs and equipment, food and water requirements, disease prevention, and collecting eggs. The handbook also contains information on breeding chickens and a list of resources for keeping chickens at home. Visit http://www.solutionsfromscience.com/?p=2077 to learn more.

## Back to Basics

*Back To Basics* is an excellent book for inspiration and instruction on how to live a simpler, more self-sufficient lifestyle. Now newly updated and including hundreds of projects, step-by-step sequences, photographs, charts, and illustrations, *Back To Basics* will show you how to do all sorts of projects, such as: dying cloth, weaving, making cheese, brewing your own beer, keeping bees, and even how to build your own log cabin! You have to see it to believe it. Visit: http://www.solutionsfromscience.com/?p=2042

## Character for Life

This amazing book contains the rich stories of some of the finest pioneers of law, politics, and religion. Over 37 different character profiles are included in the book, such as: Sojourner Truth, William Penn, Florence Nightingale, and John Marshall. Get your copy today at: http://www. solutionsfromscience.com/?p=1840

CPSIA information can be obtained at www.ICGtesting.com
Printed in the USA
LVOW110544201011

251320LV00002B/1/P